A PEOPLE'S HISTORY OF THE LAKE OF THE OZARKS

A PEOPLE'S HISTORY OF THE LAKE OF THE OZARKS

DAN WILLIAM PEEK &
KENT VAN LANDUYT

THE History PRESS

Published by The History Press
Charleston, SC
www.historypress.net

Back cover, bottom: Courtesy of Lake Area Chamber of Commerce.

First published 2016

Manufactured in the United States

ISBN 978.1.46713.550.4

Library of Congress Control Number: 2015958241

CONTENTS

ACKNOWLEDGEMENTS

The authors wish to thank all those who supported or contributed to this book, our wives and family members in particular for their patience and suffering and our intrepid text consultant, Pippa Letsky, as well as our editors at The History Press, Ben Gibson and Darcy Mahan, for their invaluable advice and assistance. The following first readers, friends, relatives and storytellers must be acknowledged, and we ask forgiveness in advance for any oversights. Thanks go to Craig Baer, Barbara Barnard, Robyn Burnette, Pat Calton, Camden County Historical Society and Museum, Joe Carter, Kathryn Cunningham, Emma Dornan, Terry and Darlene Farmer, Bob Hall, Pam Harlan, Cindy Hart, Carol Holt, Lake Area Chamber of Commerce, Joyce Mace, Maple St. Antique Mall in Eldon, Howard Wight Marshall, Miller County Historical Society and Museum, Missouri State Archives, Morgan County Historical Society and Museum, Jody Newman, Sally Oxenhandler, Lola Hook Rice, Karen Smith, Mary Stansfield, Wendy White, Kay and Lonnie Joe Williams and William W. and Dorothy Williams.

INTRODUCTION

It may still be a custom of some rural folk, as it was in earlier times, to take a plant clipping from the old homeplace when moving to a new or other place. In the Ozarks, the most common such clippings were probably that of the lilac, swaddled in mud to be planted in the soil of the next home or farmstead. Lilacs are a durable bush, and it is likely some of those born of such clippings from the lands and homes that were submerged by the creation of the Lake of the Ozarks in 1931 still blossom where the families removed came to rest.[1]

I know of this custom because it was common to my family—I am a fifth-generation Ozarker. My father's family came to the Arkansas Ozarks from Tennessee after the Civil War, in which they had sided with the South. My great-uncle Dan Peek was justice of the peace in Snowball, Arkansas, in the early twentieth century.[2]

I came of age in Morgan County, Missouri, which rims the Lake of the Ozarks. Family legend has it my father worked as a laborer in the construction of Bagnell Dam.

My mother's family name is Manes ("may-ness"). My grandfather was Daniel Boone Manes—so named as was a fairly common custom of his day. The Maneses are a Scots-Irish and Welsh clan of the sort called "Old Stock American" by some cultural historians. My branch settled in Pulaski County, Missouri, in the early decades of the nineteenth century. Two of six Manes brothers, Baptist preachers all and initially brush arborists, constructed a wooden chapel known as the "Manes Shed" in 1840. The Manes brothers were past military age when the Civil War broke out. Though Southerners, they were Unionists, and family lore states they could not bring themselves to oppose the government their parents and grandparents had fought to establish. It is said, however, their sons served in the Missouri State Guard, a Confederate militia.[3]

Some discussions or terminology in this telling of the story of the Lake of the Ozarks may be somewhat obscure or construed more of local description than by general usage and therefore require some advance notice.

Properties that front the water at the Lake of the Ozarks are often referred to as "first tier" lots. "Second tier" lots are just behind these, and "third tier" lots are those that are separated from the lake by the other tiers or by obstructions.

The designations "central Ozarks" and "interior Ozarks" as used herein refer to the regions adjacent to and on either side of the major divide or watershed (the "Ozark Divide") popularly described as the lengthy level ledge that is the roadbed of U.S. Route 63 as it passes through the Missouri Ozarks. The region host to this story—the tri-county area—is crossed by another divide running east–west generally trailing Missouri Highway 52 and the old Rock Island railroad right-of-way.

The tri-county area (also: "three-county area") consists of Missouri's Morgan, Miller and Camden Counties. The designation predates the Lake of the Ozarks and is culturally ingrained. As an example, the Tri-County Lodging Association, a promotional organization, completely ignored the existence of Benton County, which also borders the lake. Although thus separated, Benton is correctly included in geographic or academic description of the Lake of the Ozarks region.

The southwest Missouri Ozarks—the White River region and "Shepherd of the Hills Country"—is referred to as the "exterior Ozarks" in these proceedings.

The distinction between the interior Ozarks and the exterior parts is significant because although the regions share a common culture, there have been significant differences in development of infrastructure, commercial organization and the promotion of tourism.

It was the exterior Ozarks that occupied the interest of folklorists and writers of former days—the "Arcadian" view of the mountains. The contrast between the two Ozark regions can be highlighted with reference to the way these outside observers characterized the exterior Ozarks population as a "cows not plows" culture. As will be noted, the interior Ozarks of the same era—roughly mid-nineteenth century to mid-twentieth century—would aptly be described as a "hogs and logs" culture.

Also needing definition is a term employed by this narrative from the Lake of the Ozarks regional speech: "true local." This is a self-referential description that usually indicates an ancestral lineage in the lake area exceeding three generations or so. The differential is to those who arrived in the lake area after development had begun in earnest—the 1960s—and often implies these newcomers have not done right by the place and its people. It would not be incorrect to assume the term arises from a lasting sense of ambivalence if not outright animus toward the newcomers.

A NOTE ON THE WRITING OF THIS BOOK

My initial interest, which arose from research for my book *Live! At the Ozark Opry*, was concerned with the cultural and social history of the Lake of the Ozarks. But as I approached the end of a second draft, I had not yet discovered an articulation of the "key" to the description of the social organization of the lake area. The tri-county region encompasses, in square miles, an area well over the size of the state of Rhode Island. Yet there is no central regional government, and neither the state of Missouri nor the small governing entities in the area have historically made much attempt to stand in lieu.

In several ways, the Lake of the Ozarks region presents a place some Americans have come to envision as the ideal—a land where government is so limited and fragmented as to be nonexistent. Not only does such a vision defy wisdom and experience, but it also works to stymie realistic description. The first century of the lake (roughly our province herein) thus left to be described, perhaps aptly, in terms of a "Land of Oz"—with the wizard being an inscrutable "investor-owned" utility company—and laissez faire being the guiding social philosophy.

Through good fortune, I discovered a high school classmate and fellow Ozarker, Kent Van Landuyt, had authored a master's thesis in 1970 on the impact of the Lake of the Ozarks on the rural society of the region.

A sociologist, Kent had over forty years in public service with the state of Missouri and was selected by the 108th and 109th U.S. Congresses as a Congressional Fellow to provide analysis and advice on issues relating to transportation and national economic development. Our conversations on the subject of the lake and its development quickly revealed the invisible force I had not fully comprehended. The social development of the lake is ruled by, has been and is being involuntarily organized through the process—invisible to many observers—of urbanization. Of considerable interest was the fact that Kent's 1970 work had, in essence, predicted this end as inevitable. Still to be examined were the present-day results of that process and the probable future of this urban lake.

A NOTE ON THE TEXT

Where strictly personal or individual editorial comment or notice is presented, the author will be identified by initials—DWP or KVL.

Much of the foundation of this narrative is tales and conversations Kent and I and our story informants overheard as children from our parents, grandparents and neighbors—exchanges one ethnographer has characterized as "kitchen table stories." As storytellers, we are influenced by this tradition of talking and telling—an important way that cultural information and belief passes from generation to generation.

However, where possible we have sought sources, ranging from scholarly studies to popular literature and online articles, to enhance and expand the informational value of this book, which is at bottom an oral history—a "People's History," our definition of which is: "A work that not only recounts events, persons, ideas and ideals associated with specified times and the spirit of those times (*zeitgeist*) but also explores how these things were generally encountered and interpreted in vernacular experience."

In the reading, it will be useful to employ Richard R. Dohm's definition of culture: "Culture is an inclusive concept that refers to the generalized attitudes, values and orientations that distinguish one group of people from another. Political culture refers to those aspects of culture that are concerned with politically relevant objects, such as attitudes toward laws, institutions and leaders."[4]

CHAPTER 1

THE POWER OF THE FUTURE

It may have seemed a brilliant plan. Perhaps already settled sometime in the middling 1920s in his offices high in the majestic new building of the Kansas City Joint Stock Land Bank, of which he was president, Walter P. Cravens could have been thunderstricken by the flash of his own genius. As he began putting features to the scheme, Cravens might have seen that not only had he, in a singular instant, conceived of a means of breaking the grip foreclosed farm properties increasingly had on his joint stock land bank in the foreshadow of the Great Depression but also that there existed the distinct possibility that he, Walter Price Cravens, could become fabulously wealthy in the process.

It was simple. The Kansas City Joint Stock Land Bank (KCJSLB), controlled by Cravens, would trade foreclosed farms the bank owned in Kansas and Missouri for farmland and properties that were to be flooded with the construction of a hydroelectric dam on the Osage River, way down in the Ozark Mountains of Missouri. This would keep the cost and bother of annexing the land for the lake—which the dam would by necessity create—to a minimum, and it would erase the debacle of the bank's foreclosed upon farm properties, all more or less with strokes of the pen.

Supporting Cravens's scheme was the fact that much of the land bordering the Osage River was steeply mountainous rocky terrain of little value for farming or most commercial purposes. Cravens must have reckoned that the trading of such property for acreage on the tillable prairies and plains of the Kansas-Missouri region should be an easy sell.

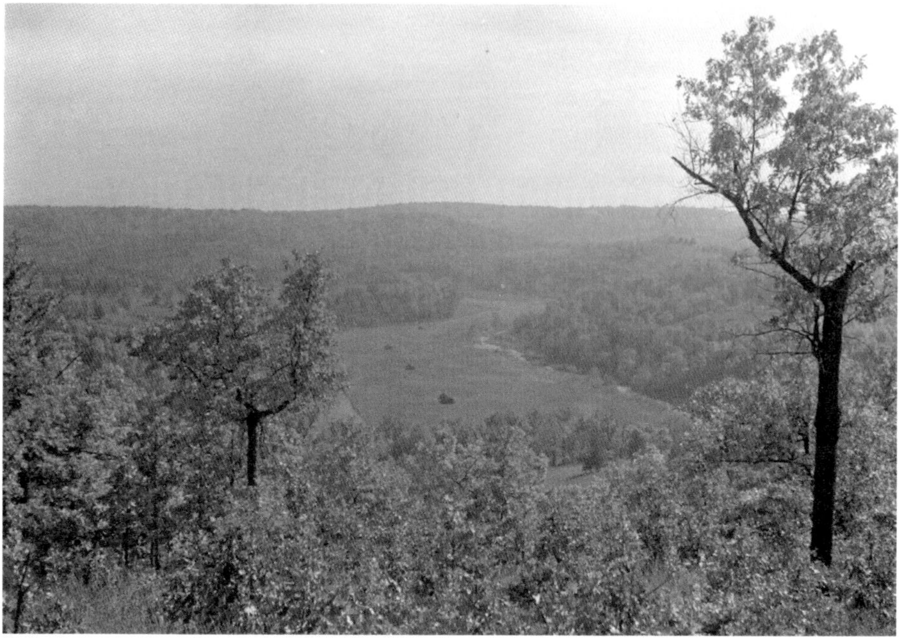

A typical section of the Osage River valley before flooding by the Bagnell Dam impoundment. *Courtesy of Missouri State Capitol Commission, Missouri State Archives.*

Of course, there was then the matter of constructing the dam and creating the lake that would flood the farmland and mountainous terrain to be traded for the foreclosed properties. But that was what would set loose the overarching opportunity in the scheme, the chance to own and operate the generation of electricity to the urban centers, in particular, St. Louis—not to mention a huge private sporting and recreational lake—all to be owned by Cravens or entities under his control.[1]

In the 1920s, following the passage of the Federal Water Power Act, electricity was a brisk commodity, and the race to generate and distribute the power of the future was of great interest to America's commercial culture.

This interest played right into Cravens's grand scheme, since he did not have anywhere near the $30 million the United States Eighth Circuit Court of Appeals would later hazard as the amount he would have needed to build what would become Bagnell Dam and to create the Lake of the Ozarks. (The final cost is sometimes reported as $36 million—the early twenty-first-century multiplier was said to be $300 to $360 million.)

The idea of constructing a hydroelectric dam on the Osage River was not original to Walter Cravens. Reports usually credit the inspiration to

Ralph Street, a Kansas City lawyer who had begun searching for the means to do so in 1912.

In any case, Street and Cravens would enter into an ill-fated partnership of sorts in 1924 with the aim of fulfilling Street's plans for the Osage River.

Hydroelectric dams were not an untested concept. Such dams of limited utility had been constructed as early as the 1880s, and in 1913, the White River, in the southwestern Missouri Ozarks, had been successfully subdued by the "Powersite Dam." Its flood, the first of the created Ozark lakes, known as "Lake Taneycomo" (a reference of place: Taney County Missouri). The differences between conditions and culture surrounding the White River project and the Osage River damming are significant and will be discussed later in this narrative.

With nigh a century hindsight, the very idea of Cravens and Street conspiring to somehow make something so grand out of nothing—which as we will see, is pretty much what the two actually had between them in relation to what their dam scheme would demand—seems strange to say the

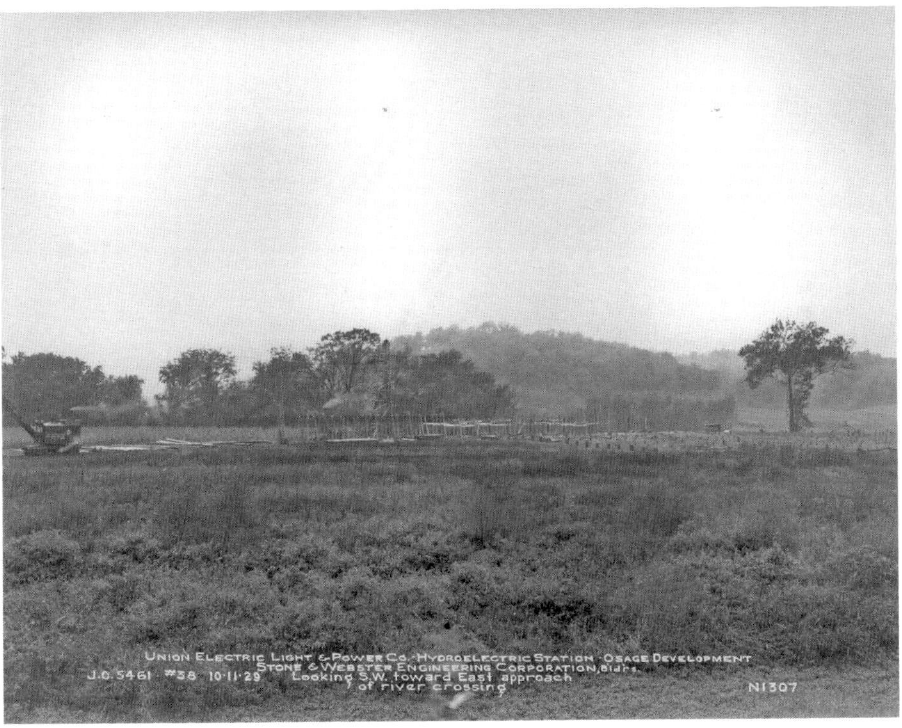

Construction started on October 11, 1929—an action that forever changed lifestyles in the Ozarks. *Courtesy of Missouri State Capitol Commission, Missouri State Archives.*

least. But it was, after all, the Roaring Twenties; the "War to End All Wars" had been fought and won, and the times were rapidly changing.

Although the date depends somewhat on how the terms "urban" and "rural" are defined, 1925 is often pegged as the year in which half of the American population became urbanites—a statistic of importance to this story. Many of the urban population in those days, though, would have come of age on farms or in rural regions and thus had perhaps retained a sense of ancestral rural customs and values even as they migrated to city days and ways.[2]

Street and Cravens were both urban denizens, and the question is begged how much either man knew about the Ozarks and the hill folk, whom they apparently expected to cooperate fully, without question and passively, with them in their great Osage River scheme.

CHAPTER 2

YOU CAN'T GET THERE FROM HERE

As the Osage impoundment scheme of Street and Cravens is considered, it seems more and more likely that neither man truly had much conception of the culture and contests they were about to experience in the Ozark Mountains.

The logistics alone should have given reason to pause. Even two and a half decades into the twentieth century, the central Ozarks environs encompassed daunting isolation, transportation uncertain at best and paved roads nonexistent in much of the region until after mid-century.

The major non-rail land thoroughfare of the Ozarks for much of the nineteenth century had been the Telegraph Road, or "Old Wire Road," which for a good stretch followed ancient traces tramped out by Native American tribes. The main trace shadowed the Missouri River out of St. Louis and eventually fell into the path of a long cut through the forests needed for the stringing of telegraph lines, accomplished at the time of the Civil War. The Telegraph Road terminated at Fort Smith, Arkansas.[1]

As far as roads that would accept fine carriages or automobiles, the interior Ozarks of the late nineteenth and early twentieth centuries were a hard way to go. And daily life was of the same rugged character.

A recollection of nineteenth-century life in those mountains appeared in the *Versailles Statesman* newspaper in 1927. (The town name is pronounced "Vur-Sales," and it is Morgan County's seat of government.) The interviewee is Monroe Ivy, referred to in the article as General Ivy, and the title of the piece is "Gen Monroe Ivy, over 80, Looks Backward Sixty Years and Sees Things to Talk About."

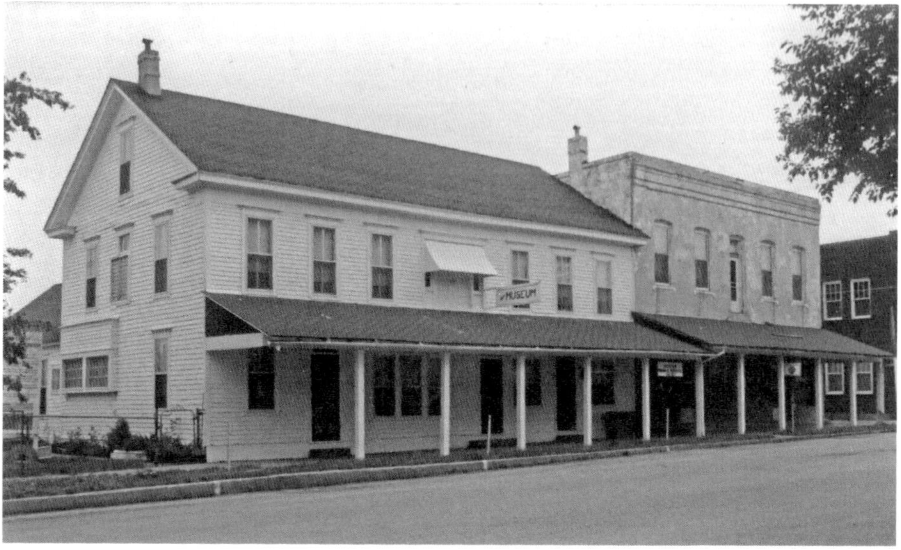

The Martin Hotel in downtown Versailles dates back to the 1850s. The hotel records list Civil War–era visitors, and the hotel was also a stagecoach stop. Now the hotel is the home of Morgan County Historical Society and Museum. It has been designated as a National Historic Site. *Courtesy of Morgan County Historical Society.*

The "General" was born in 1843. He lived to be ninety-three years of age and a valued and highly regarded citizen of Morgan County. As a matter of information, "General" was a respectful community honorific. Ivy served in the Confederate army under Major General J.S. Marmaduke and saw action in a number of the bloody skirmishes characteristic of the war in Missouri. He once related that the Battle of Pilot Knob was the only major conflict in which he participated.

Pertinent to this segment is the General's recount of how meat was procured in the Ozarks of his time:

> *He said hogs ran wild in the woods and grew to be five and six years old in many cases. He said more hogs died of starvation in the winter time than is consumed in that section now. Hog prices were so low and shipping facilities were so poor that it did not pay to care for the hogs. They fed on the mass* [sic] *in the late fall, developed some fat and men would go to the woods and kill what they wanted and bring it in like bringing in a mass* [sic] *of squirrels. Cattle grew wild in the woods and died in the winter about the same way.*[2]

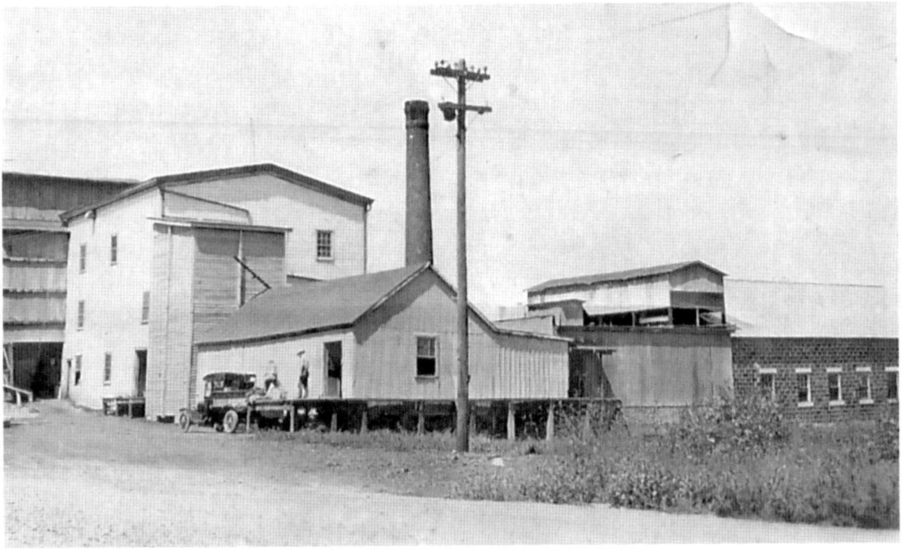

A photo of the Versailles Ice and Coal Plant. The city generated its own electric power because there were no other electricity providers in the area. The tall stack in the background is the power plant. *Courtesy of Morgan County Historical Society.*

The word "mass" was incorrectly apprehended or transcribed in both cases in the quoted passage. The first word should be "mast," which is the fruit or seeds of trees that fall to the ground. The last is certainly "mess"—in the Ozarks, three or more slaughtered squirrels would have been referred to in this way.

Human life in the north central Ozarks in the late nineteenth and early twentieth centuries was often that of isolation and a "hunter-gatherer" sustenance system with very little other support. As General Ivy noted, there was no physical infrastructure to sustain commercial or agricultural efforts of any significance.

By the twenty-first century, the Ozarks would yield plentiful wild greens and berries most years. Paw paws ("Ozark bananas") thrived in some locales. (That fruit, though, is a favorite of wild turkeys—said to be tough competitors for its consumption.) But as the nineteenth century progressed to a close, much of the wild abundance of the Ozarks had become starvation scarce. At the dawn of the twentieth century, the population of wild game—in particular, deer—in the Missouri Ozarks had been slaughtered past the point of extirpation.[3]

To know that a hardscrabble way of life was forced on the earlier inhabitants of the Ozarks by mountainous isolation and lack of transport, among other factors, is extremely important in understanding the society of the interior Ozarks.

It is likely the time under discussion in this chapter—the nineteenth and early twentieth centuries—is when a negative stereotype began to attach to Ozarkers. And the old-stock Ozark hunter-gatherer tradition, as more and more outsiders observed it, came to be viewed by the general culture as a trait of a people too lazy to engage in traditional farming or to work at modern occupations.

This was and is a misconception of the culture, but Ozark society, as will be seen, does not always assist outsiders in understanding mountain folkways.

As noted, the old-time Ozark ideas of access of property or livestock were more matters of custom and usage than of plat or pen. And the skill sets of mountain survival could be viewed by outsiders as primitive or even bizarre; "noodling," for example—catching fish by hand—is an activity long practiced in the region.

The traditional Ozark life of isolation and hardship infused a fierce personal pride and independence that is still often evident and will weave consistently through this story.

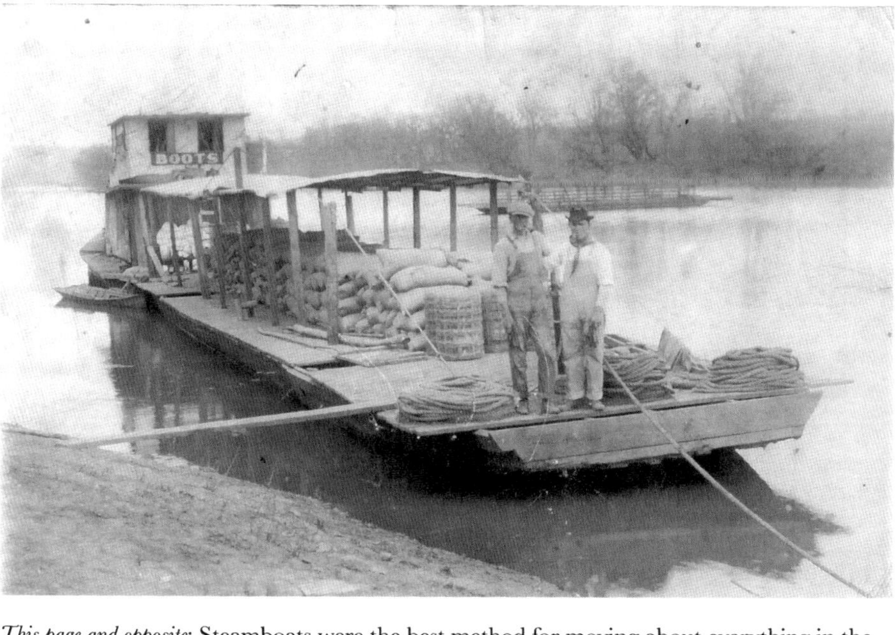

This page and opposite: Steamboats were the best method for moving about everything in the Ozarks, along the Osage River. The absence of all-season roads and limited rail service made the Osage River "king of transportation" for many years. These photos show the variety of boats in use in the early 1900s. *Courtesy of Miller County Missouri Historical Society.*

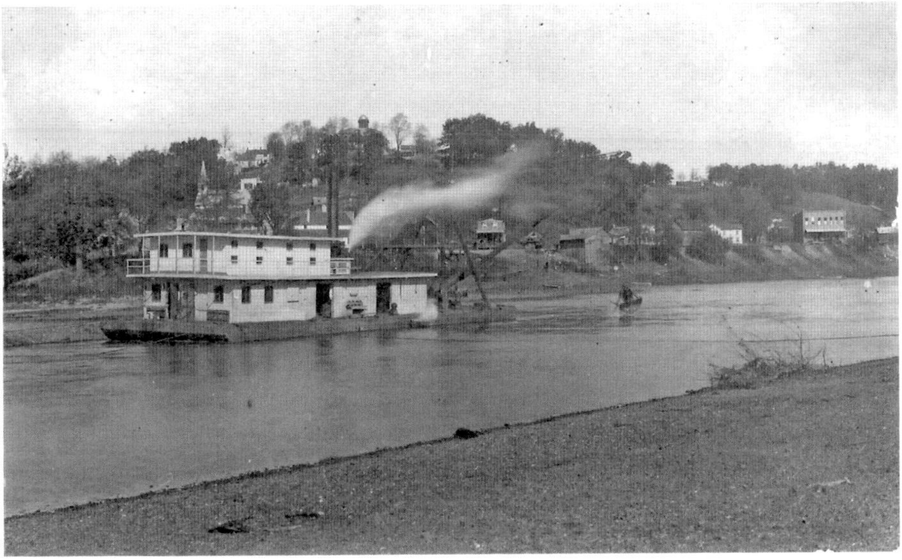

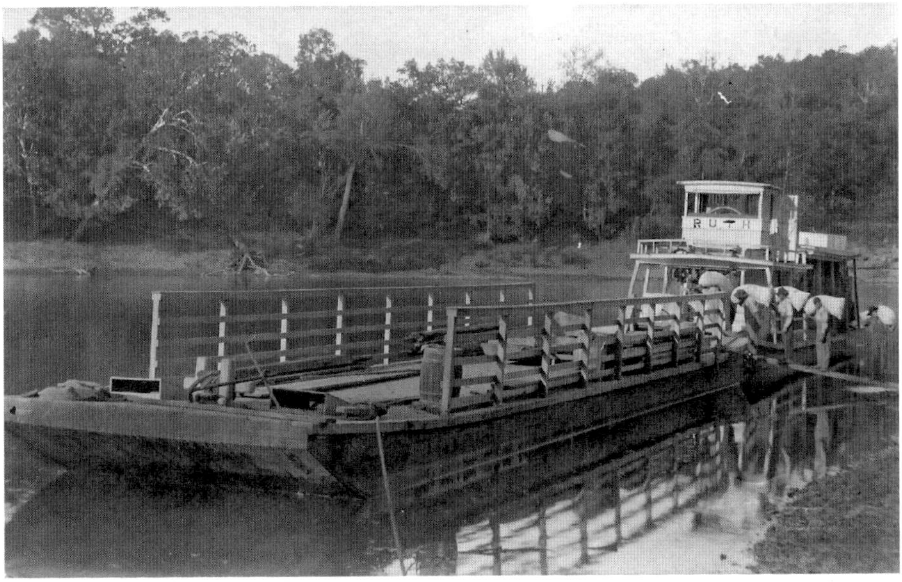

Daniel Woodrell perfectly expressed this engrained ferocity of pride in the cultural character in his book *Winter's Bone,* set deep in the Missouri Ozarks. In one passage, the protagonist, Ree Dolly, is asked by her younger brother if a relative is going to share some food, which they desperately need, and says, "Could be we should ask." Ree twists his ear for emphasis and admonishes him, "*Never*. Never ask for what ought to be offered."

During much of the nineteenth century, the principal means of transport for commerce in the north central interior Ozarks were small steam-powered and diesel-powered riverboats that plied the Osage River and other navigable streams of the region. These were precarious vessels of perilous draft and ill-tempered engines of the type referenced in the old song "Saro Jane" ("The whistle gave a squall and the engineer blew through a hole in the wall").[4]

Put simply, most means of mass or mechanized land transportation in the central interior Ozarks terminated or skirted abruptly at the foothills until well into the twentieth century.

The Missouri Pacific Railroad, for example, completed a line designated the "Boonville-Versailles Branch" in 1880. But Versailles is located at the exact juncture of a broad plateau stretching to the Missouri River from the Ozark upland—immediately north and west of the town is prairie, immediately south is mountainous. The rail company did not attempt any ascension there.

Versailles, Missouri historian Dorothy Bartram wrote, "A big celebration was held in Versailles in observance of the completion of the railroad line on June 2 of that year. A great crowd of Morgan Countians, some of whom had never seen a train, were on hand to see the arrival of the first train in Versailles."

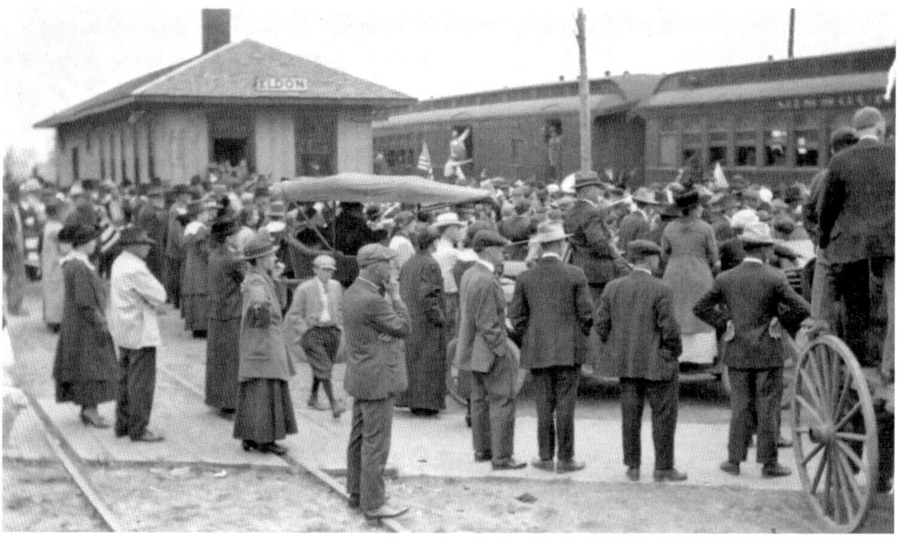

An early twentieth-century photo of a crowd meeting the Missouri Pacific train in Eldon. This train continued south to the Bagnell community. *Courtesy of Miller County Missouri Historical Society.*

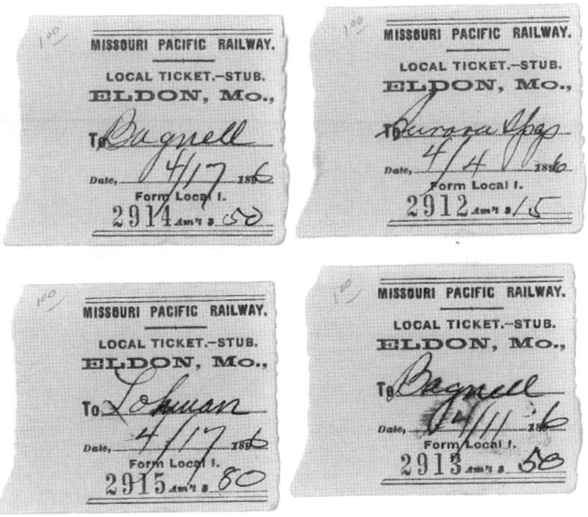

Left: Actual 1896 ticket stubs for the Eldon branch of Missouri Pacific Railroad. *Author's private collection (KVL).*

Below: Early photo of the Eldon Rock Island Railroad Depot. This Rock Island line ran between Kansas City and St. Louis. This Eldon Rock Island Depot was the impetus for the famous TV show *Petticoat Junction. Courtesy of Miller County Missouri Historical Society.*

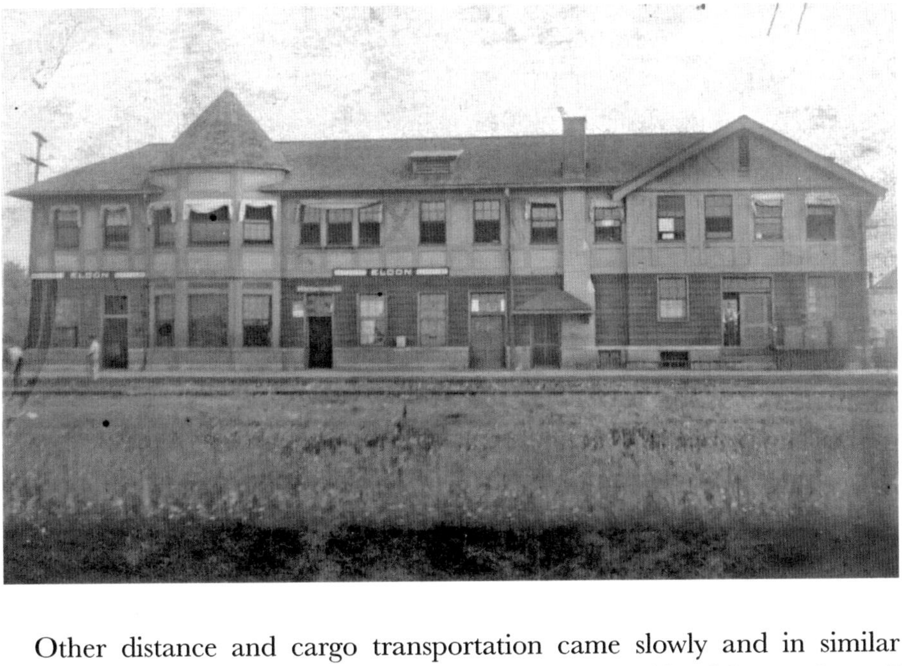

Other distance and cargo transportation came slowly and in similar manner to the region. But in 1884, the Missouri Pacific did extend a rail line from Jefferson City deeper into the interior Ozarks, and the town of Bagnell, an import and export point for livestock and goods, expanded quickly around the railhead there.

In a privately recorded interview in 1987, Mason Roseborough "Doc" Foster, a well-known Ozarks (Camden County) raconteur, recollected that well into the twentieth century, livestock drives from the surrounding mountains to the Bagnell station were common. He noted that the drives were of both cattle and hogs.[5]

Circa 1905, the Rock Island Railroad established a terminus at Eldon, Missouri. It is an event still celebrated in that Ozarks town, though that railway did not attempt to breach the Ozark Mountains.

As the twentieth century progressed, more rail transport came to the Ozarks, but there was still a considerable question of whether it was possible to "get there from here," as was posed by an old Ozarks witticism.

CHAPTER 3

HOGS AND LOGS

All the men in the 1987 video refered to in the final paragraphs of the previous chapter (produced by Joyce Mace and the Lee Mace's Ozark Opry organization) were participants in the construction of Bagnell Dam or the development and promotion of the Lake of the Ozarks shoreline as property. Doc Foster, as example, was hired by Ralph Street in the mid-1920s to assist a local surveyor, Ralph Vincent, in the "benchmarking" of the region to be flooded—which is to say marking by various means the 660 plus line above sea level, the lake's proposed depth.

Foster was born in 1909 on a farm northeast of Old Linn Creek; Al Elam was born in 1911 in Ralls County. A graduate of the Rolla School of Mines (renamed "Missouri University of Science and Technology"), Elam came to the lake area in 1936 with the Missouri Highway Department as a civil engineer assigned to rebuild the rerouted Highway 54 after the dam flood. Ernest McNeil—a cousin to Doc Foster—was born in 1900 in what was then the Indian Territories, now the state of Oklahoma. Carl Williams and James Franklin Sr. were both born in the 1920s in what would become the lake region. Franklin was an influential local banker and a close associate of Carl Williams. Williams was Lee Mace's brother-in-law and owned supermarkets in the Osage Beach area. Mace, who died in 1985, was the founder of the Ozark Opry and an active entrepreneur and promoter. Carl Williams dedicated the 1987 video to Lee Mace.

Taken as a whole, the panel assembled for the 1987 video well represented authentic source memory of the early history of the Lake of the Ozarks.

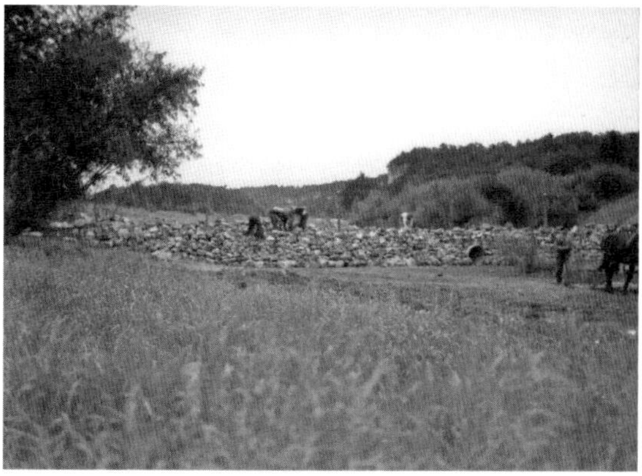

Left: Building a dike and temporary crossing in the Osage River valley. *Courtesy of Missouri State Capitol Commission, Missouri State Archives.*

Below: The construction company built bunk houses for the dam construction workers on a hilltop located on the east side of the dam site. *Courtesy of Missouri State Capitol Commission, Missouri State Archives.*

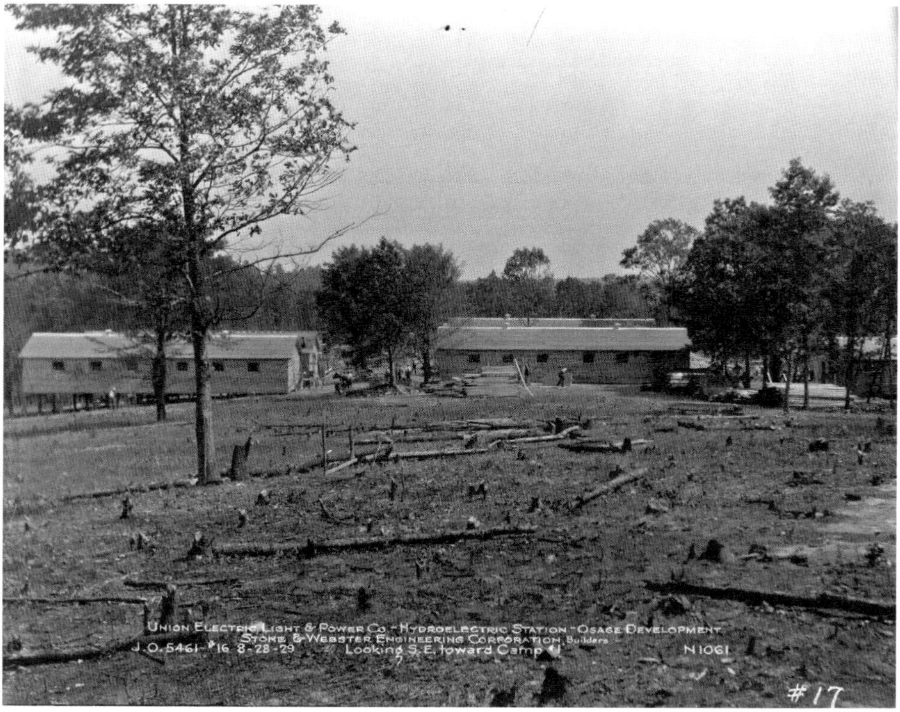

These men could be described as the original "true locals" of the tri-county area, and their memories extended well back beyond the lake.

The old-time descriptions provided by General Ivy (in the 1927 newspaper article) and Doc Foster (in the 1987 video) may summon comparisons to similar approaches to animal husbandry in the more exterior lands of the Ozark Mountains and on the prairies and grasslands in the western United States—the "open range."

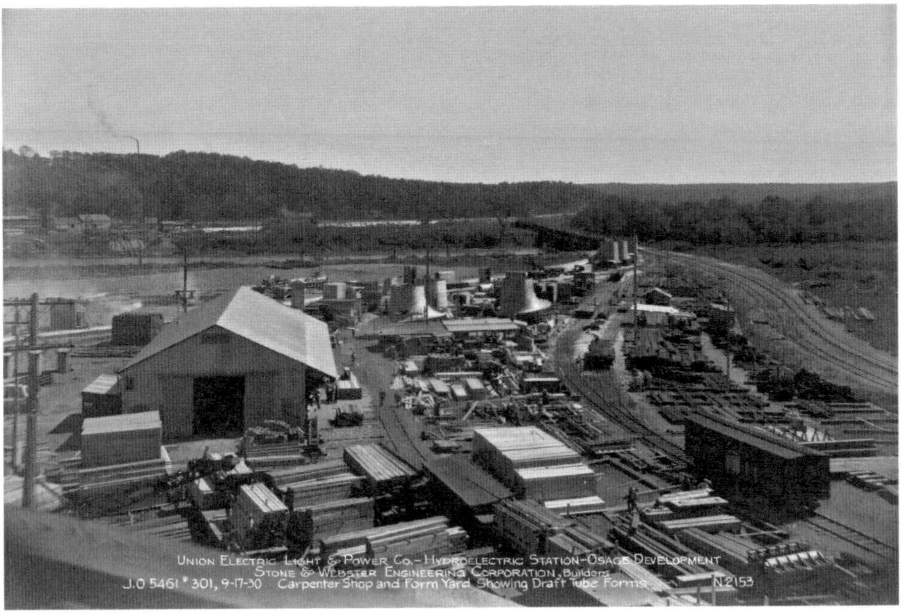

A construction site carpenter shop. *Courtesy of Missouri State Capitol Commission, Missouri State Archives.*

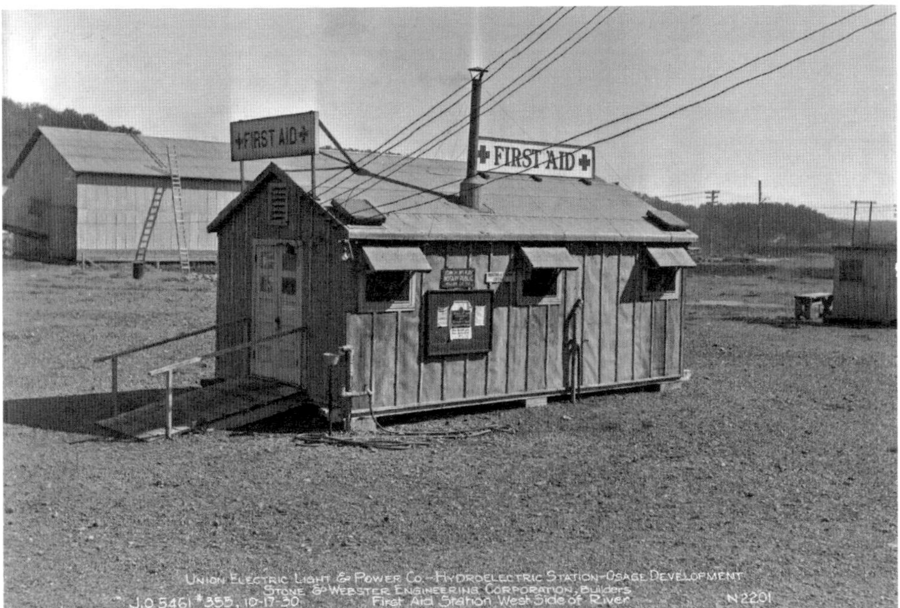

A construction site first aid building. *Courtesy of Missouri State Capitol Commission, Missouri State Archives.*

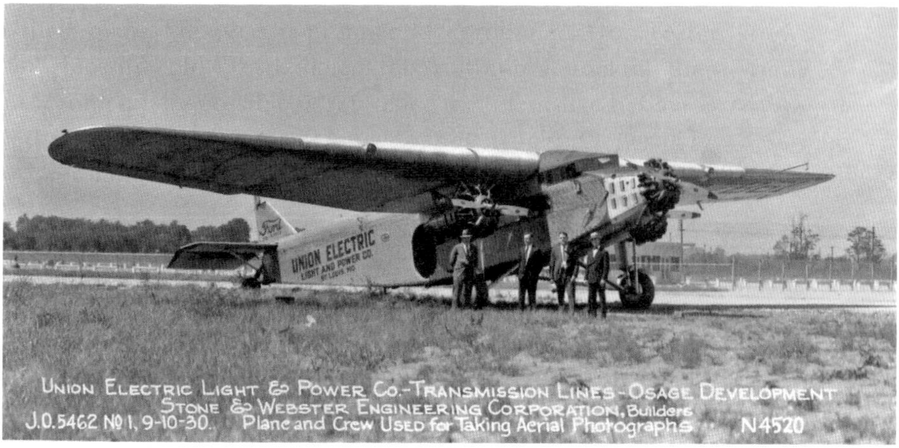

Aerial photography was conducted regularly by this plane over the entire project. *Courtesy of Missouri State Capitol Commission, Missouri State Archives.*

The primary difference may be that in the latter nineteenth-century north central Ozarks referenced by Ivy, the livestock—almost all hogs—ran free and were available to any inhabitant who could bring them down. In the farms and ranches to the west, much of the stock were cattle that did range free but customarily bore their owner's brand. The husbandry was transhumant, and to appropriate branded livestock for any reason was generally considered a crime.

Topography alone (geographic determinism) may have dictated some of this difference. Herding livestock across mountainous terrain and turgid streams may have been a bit more difficult than rounding them up out on the western range—but that's a topic for buckaroos to debate and to be left at that.

It would be a grievous error to believe Ozarkers could be deterred by any particular difficulty or that, as the popular image of Ozarkers would eventually come to portray, they lacked industriousness. In fact, the Ozarks hill folk of the late nineteenth and early twentieth centuries seem in some ways the very picture of industry—perhaps a little too much so by twenty-first-century ecological standards.

The March 2011 issue of *Missouri Conservationist* published an interesting article on the Missouri Ozark Forest Ecosystem Project—a discussion of "forest management practices and their effect on flora and fauna." The article contemplates a question first raised in 1989: whether "clear-cut harvests in extensive, mature forests, like those found in the Ozarks increase cowbird parasitism."

The cowbird question is explored in the article (but will not be discussed here). Then a historical perspective is offered on the Ozark forests in general—note that the article dates the end of the great "tie hacker" clear-cut at about 1929.

The Missouri Ozark Forest Ecosystem Project is distractingly referred to in the article by the acronym MOFEP. Where the acronym appears, it may be helpful to read as if it were instead the full title of the project—as has been first inserted, for clarification, in the quote below:

> *The MOFEP* [Missouri Ozark Forest Ecosystem Project] *sites, like most of the Missouri Ozarks, are second-growth forests, a repercussion of the area's turn-of-the-20th-century vast timber harvest, in which first short leaf pine, and then oaks and hickories were heavily cut. Because the forest essentially sprouted from this early 20th century clear-cut, most of MOFEP's mature trees were 60 to 80 years old at the projects inception in 1989. Faster-growing red oak group species like black oak and scarlet oak (24 and 21 percent of all trees on MOFEP land respectively) now dominate the forest, and in accordance with typical 100-year life spans of the red oak group are nearing maturity. Among younger trees, however, white oak trees dominate the forest (currently 21 percent of all trees in MOFEP). White oak trees number nearly twice that of black and scarlet oak, because they grow better in shade.*[1]

The article makes no further mention of the great clear-cut of the Ozarks forest—largely a result of the industry provisioning wooden railroad ties ("tie hackers") during the height of America's era of railroad expansion. Note that the article identifies the favored tie timber—shortleaf pine, oaks and hickories.

Here is a description by Howard Wight Marshall, the prominent Missouri cultural historian, of the rail tie industry as it was pursued on the flatlands in the northern part of the state:

> *After the Civil War, itinerant laborers did much of the wooden tie and timber production in Northern Missouri, hewing railroad ties with broad axes in the intermittent expanses of white oak forest. The richness and extent of the old growth timber, though accented by grasslands, meant that hard wood stock for ties, bridge construction, and the like was available near the lines. The laborers cleared the right of way, prepared roadbed, laid track and performed other jobs.*

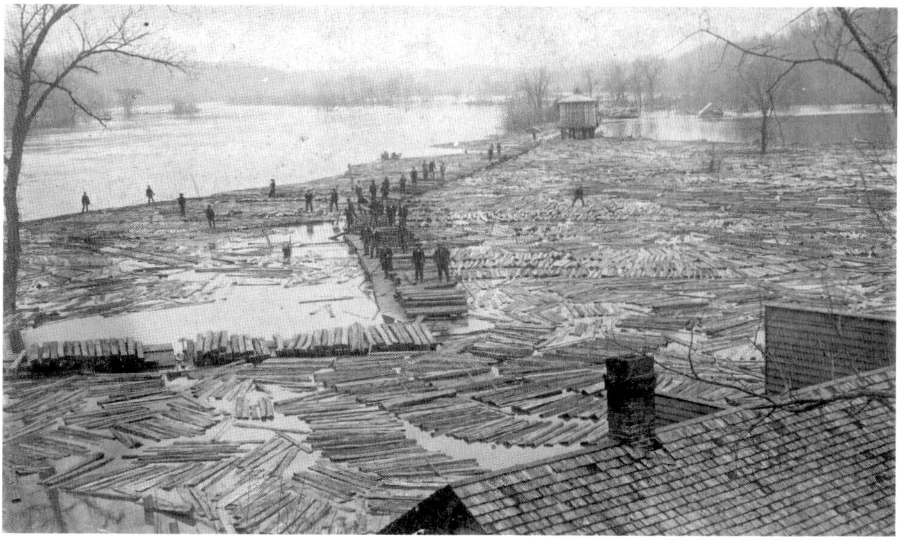

Tie cutting was a major livelihood for native Ozarkians in the last part of the nineteenth century and first part of the twentieth century. Railroads were the "king of transportation," and demand was high for the railroad ties. The abundance of the Ozarks native hardwoods provided a good income source. The trees were cut, owner marked, moved to the hillside and launched into the river. The ties were guided downriver like a herd of animals. This photo shows a lot of ties and high water. Perhaps the high water helped in moving a vast number of ties at one time. *Courtesy of Missouri State Capitol Commission, Missouri State Archives.*

Tie hackers abounded in the Ozarks also, but it was a markedly different enterprise—the labor was local and the logistics considerably more challenging than that of the prairie of Missouri's Little Dixie and northern plains regions.

Once the Ozark timber was felled, the issue became how to get the ties from mountain to market. The solution was "log rolling"—the term means doing everything from actually rolling to finding the balance point to perch the log on a shoulder and carry it to whatever land conveyance was in use or just manhandling the subject tree trunk along until a stream or river could be found. There was a "log slide" at Hurricane Deck and a similar depot at Linn Creek; once in the water, ties were fashioned into huge rafts and floated downriver to the next means to get them to market.

This was by no stretch a sure method to transport the product. Although the logs had an owner's mark burned or stamped into the stump ends, if a tie raft broke up, it was a simple matter for log poachers along the river to retrieve the loose ties, trim off the owner's brand and simply replace it with their own. This was a practice, according to Doc Foster, known as "rattin'" (possibly old Ozark dialect for "righting"—making them "right" or "legal"—or, equally possible, a reference to rodent-like behavior).[2]

In the previously cited 1927 newspaper article, General Ivy described how "log rollings" were carried out:

> *When talking of these old days General Ivy looked away into space like one in dreams and shook his head, saying: "many happy days in the old time. Everyone was honest neighborly and helpful." When asked how many men usually attended these log rollings on his place that took two or three days the General said: "sometimes there would be sixty or seventy men and lots of women would come along to be at the 'Big Doings' and we would have a great time."*

CHAPTER 4

OZARKIANA ATTITUDE

Reviewing the local histories, personal transcriptions and reports of the interior Ozark culture of the late nineteenth and early to mid-twentieth centuries reveals a society of good and generous neighbors, as General Ivy described. However, gun and knife fights to settle personal or familial feuds were fairly common, and drunken fisticuffs were a regular form of community entertainment. Much of this entertainment was, according to various accounts, provided by older bachelor men who lived reclusive lives but came into town every so often to get liquored up, unruly and, ultimately, jailed.

Ernest McNeil related the story of one such recluse, J.R. Miller, who rode into town on his mule from his house in Shawnee Bend every half year or so for the purpose of drinking liquor at the local grocery-saloon. This was sometime in the second decade of the twentieth century. McNeil noted, "All the old men in those days rode mules," to which Doc Foster added, "Or stud horses."

Whenever Miller was taken in for the inevitable drunken brawl, young people would go to the jail to visit and be entertained. Miller would rattle the barred cell door and yell at them:

Here I am, John R. Miller, the flower of Shawnee Bend
A thousand cows upon a thousand hills
Money to loan and money to spend
And here I am in jail with a damned *n****r*

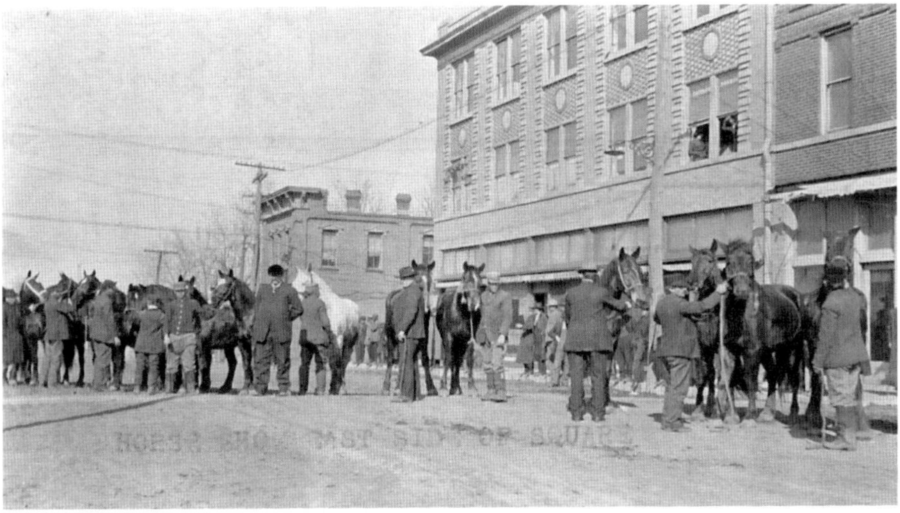

Missourians are proud of their mules and work horses. This is a photo of a local horse and mule show on the square in downtown Versailles. *Courtesy of Morgan County Historical Society.*

(The racially charged language is included herein with great reluctance and repugnance. However, this is a recounting of cultural history and, as such, demands unflinching candor in such matters.)

The chant was apparently Miller's signature with the townspeople—"The Flower of Shawnee Bend," indeed.

On the subject of brawling as community pastime and spectator sport, McNeil said the most intense such activity always occurred on Christmas Eve and the Fourth of July. He noted that those dates were when the fighting was most likely to turn deadly, with no holds barred and often entailing what he referred to as "cuttin' contests."

In addition to brawls and feuds, it seems that in the Ozarks of old, almost everything—including sexual assignations, adultery and incest—was carried out, by necessity, more or less openly. This is another characteristic that has attached to the regions "hillbilly" mythology: that of a sexually amoral society. That imagery has been forwarded by writers like Vance Randolph and Donald Harington, among others.

Bill and Dorothy Williams, Morgan County's dedicated historians, tell of socializing on the square in Versailles during the 1930s, when Bill was a teenager working at the local grocery. He recalled, "Everybody came to the Square on Saturday night and there went to their usual spots—if you wanted to see someone in particular you knew where to find them."

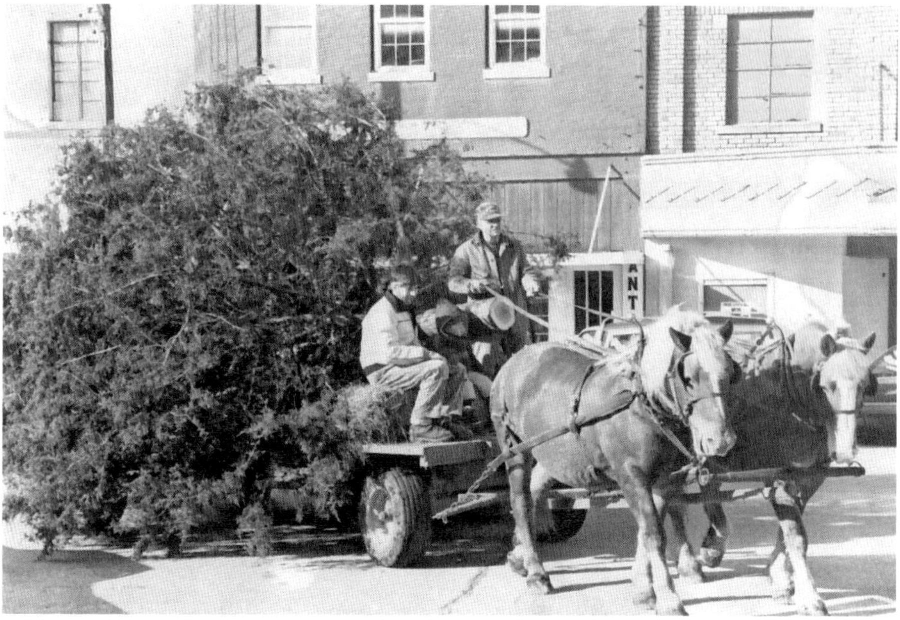

The Christmas holidays are very important in Ozark towns. The large tree is brought into Versailles via a wagon and team. The tree will be put on the north side of the courthouse lawn and decorated, and residents have a ceremonial lighting on the Thanksgiving weekend. *Courtesy of Kay and Lonnie Joe Williams.*

One of the locals was carrying on an adulterous affair and would meet his paramour at the grocery where Bill Williams worked on Saturday nights. Everybody in the county knew about it, and the adulterer's wife made her business to be elsewhere on the square while it was going on. What may seem remarkable is that the adulterer openly discussed the shenanigans with the youthful Williams.

Williams recalled the man coming to the grocery one Saturday and, while waiting for his partner to drive up, revisited a sermon from the previous Sunday—a blistering review of the sanctity of marriage and the sin of adultery.

"There I sat," the man told Williams, "in the front row, a pillar of the church—and guilty as sin."

Much has been written of the music of the Ozarks. Jack Hurst in the introduction to his book *Nashville's Grand Ole Opry* wrote that the Ozarks (of the 1920s) was the "region and era that inspired the Grand Ole Opry."

Prior to the age of live radio music in the 1920s or so, there were few steady paying jobs for musicians in the mountains. Most families had members who played musical instruments, and some played for neighborhood house parties called "play parties" in the old times. By the mid-twentieth century, they were "music parties" and, by the late twentieth century, "jams." But music making in the old days was considered separate from "work" and thus not eligible for wages or fees. Joyce Mace recalled that her father played the fiddle but only at home. Perhaps there will always be those Ozarkers who would agree with the statement: "I like a man playing the fiddle—but he shouldn't get paid for it."

Missouri and Ozarks culture are also famous for the high regard in which mules have historically been held. The mule has a unique ability to place its rear hoofs in the exact places in which its front hoofs have trod. This makes for a sure-footed steed in traversing mountainous terrain. This trait also made the mule a preferred plow animal. Old-timers speaking of their favorite mules almost always noted something to the effect of "that animal never stepped on a (crop) plant."

Then there is the relationship Ozarkers maintain with fire. It is not uncommon to see a "burn pile" in the front or side yard of a rural house or even those of Ozark country towns (though some towns require a "burn permit"). It is by bonfire that unwanted or discarded things are disposed of in this culture.

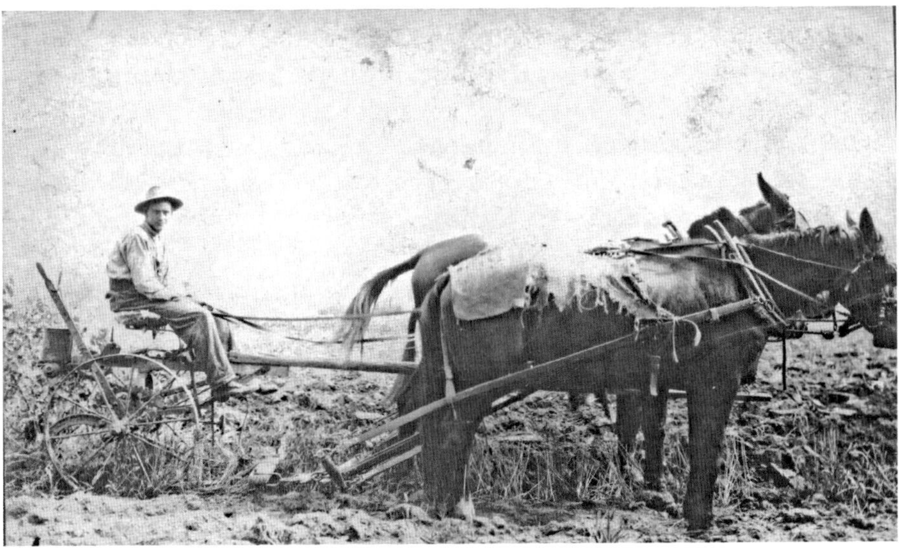

A team pulling a plow is another example of farming the Ozarks bottomland. Look closely—there are three horses or mules hooked to this single plow. *Courtesy of Miller County Missouri Historical Society.*

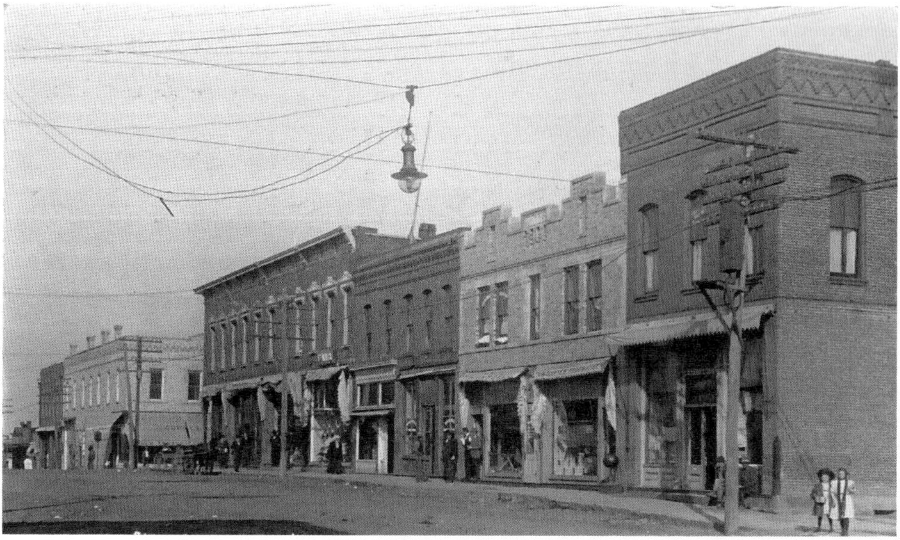

The north side of the Versailles square, across the street from the Morgan County Courthouse, housed a bank, a drugstore, a jewelry store and a dry goods store. This early 1900 photo also shows the overhead electric lines. *Courtesy of Morgan County Historical Society.*

Ozarks tracts of grasses and vegetation are burned off in the springtime and autumn. Usually, areas around dwellings (but at times also field range and forest floor) are put ablaze in these deliberately set grass fires. The general explanation for this practice is that it makes for healthier vegetation growth in the coming season, and sometimes natural debris in ditches and culverts is burned off. Another older form of the practice is said to require burning right up to the cabin. This was explained as a means of controlling insect and varmint populations.

Whatever reason the fire is started, it not infrequently spreads beyond the desired perimeters and takes down fence rows, outbuildings, barns, dwelling places and other unintended targets. During the month of March, Ozarks fire departments respond to scores of grass fires.

Richard Rhodes, writing on the subject of the Ozarks, pinned the "burning off" practice to the strength of culture:

> *The first Americans to go into the area, hunter-farmers from Kentucky and Tennessee, thinned out the wild game and girdled the trees to kill them so that they could plant corn. They believed that the humus on the forest floor inhibited the growth of grass, as indeed it did, and they began informal*

programs of annual burning that destroyed the primary source of organic matter available to improve the thin, rocky Ozark soil.

Humus is the natural material from which soil forms. Its exact nature is not well understood. The Missouri Department of Conservation has spoken plainly to the effects of the burn-off tradition: "Fires set each spring were meant to encourage herbaceous growth for livestock forage but only added to the ecological devastation" in the old-time "free range" and "clear cut" days of the Ozarks.

Gerard Schultz places the custom far back in regional history, writing that the Indians used seasonal burns to clear land for crops and others to drive game animals toward their hunting parties. The implication may be that the early settlers learned the practice from their Native American precedents. Centuries later, many Ozarkers continued the "informal programs of annual burning"—by then possibly a culturally ingrained ritual—celebrating the turn of the seasons as much as any other stated purposes.

The old Ozark custom of planting crops according to the phases of the moon or other natural signs has also been viewed by some outside observers as cultural ritual or superstition. However, such custom is most likely the product of a centuries-old "oral almanac," extant long before modern agricultural studies and practices. As Leonard Hall wrote on this subject: "The connection between agriculture and astrology is ancient beyond the records of man and may, for all we know, have considerable foundation in fact."

Another characteristic that was noted by students of Ozarks culture is the practice by older men of the mountains of telling long, generally pointless stories.

(DWP:) These products were, it has been said, called "Windies" and may be still. I am relating from personal experience. My grandfather (born in the 1880s) was a master of the art in his elder years. He would take a grandchild on his knee, gather round the remainder of the children or others available for audience, hook a thumb in the bib of his overalls, lean back, close his eyes and launch into a lengthy story about old-time days on the railroad or some other experiences that seemed likely fuel for a good fable but were, in the end, woven into aimless narratives terminating abruptly at the junction of Nowhere and What the Hay.

Family members—notably my sister Lola Hook Rice and a cousin, Cindy Hart—state that the cultural drill down of this tradition is far greater than may be immediately apparent. The subtexts were often to first determine

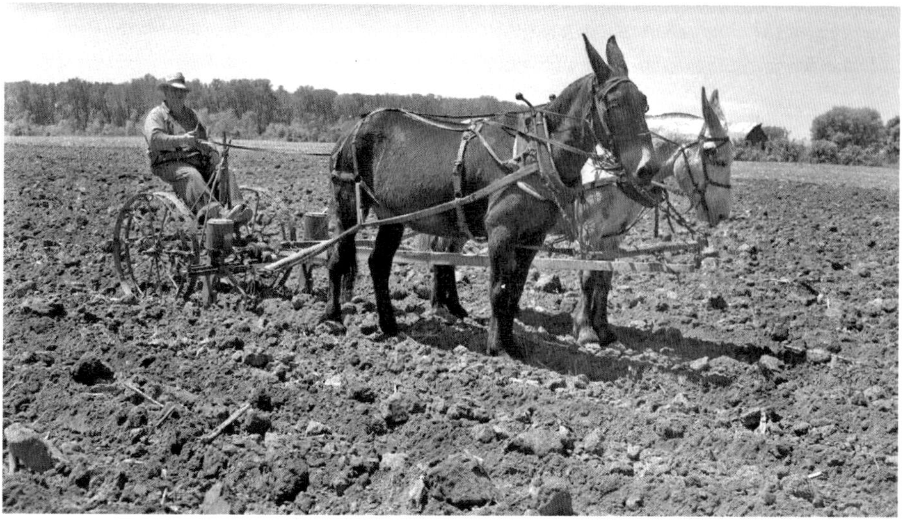

This team of mules, pulling a corn planter, represents a very common method of farming the Ozarks bottomland. *Courtesy of Missouri State Capitol Commission, Missouri State Archives.*

the audience's relationship to the community (did they recognize the story references) and next to discover if there was any blood—or blood feud—relationship between the parties. And apparently some of the "Windies" were traditionalized narratives, and the nonsensical finales depended on whether or when the storyteller lost track of which tale was involved in the telling and slugged in a piece or two of another such story.

Then there was the fondness of Ozarkers for Walmart stores (during the time of this narrative). To favor Walmart had long been considered by some segments of the American general culture to signify a lack of shopping sophistication. Walmart, however, was a store that was founded by Ozarkers, of the Ozarks and for Ozarkers. James "Bud" Walton—Sam Walton's brother and co-founder of the Walmart chain—owned a five-and-dime in Versailles for a number of years, and the Walmart headquarters is located in the Arkansas Ozarks where Sam originally operated a "dime" store.[1]

The chain's rural roots were one of the reasons for its success. While the more urban discounters generally had conflicted marketing strategies with regard to location or destination, Sam Walton apparently knew very well that in rural regions, everything is a destination. Thus was avoided the temptation to pay premium for location as the enterprise grew.

Chapter 5

A Federal Case

The tale of the joint stock land banks of the early twentieth century may seem alarmingly familiar to informed Americans.

The land bank program was twin tiered, both engaged in the grant of farm mortgages. One tier, the federal land banks, was operated by the federal government and had the mission of assuring that smaller borrowers were adequately serviced. There were twelve federal land banks established, capitalized at a minimum of $750,000 each and offering farm loans of five to forty years in duration.[1]

The second tier, known as joint stock land banks (JSLBs), was private shareholder corporations, which were, by law, supposed to be subject to supervision by the federal government. But in pre–Great Depression days, such supervision was ill defined or so under-enforced as to be meaningless. The joint stock land banks provide an excellent example of the consequences of lack of government oversight and regulation.

The joint stock land banks were purposed with making larger farm mortgage loans. They were chartered to finance these loans by selling tax-free bonds and required capitalization of $250,000.

On December 31, 1929, the average joint stock land bank loan was reported to be $6,044, and the average federal land bank loan was $2,925.

The JSLBs were chartered by the Federal Farm Loan Act of 1916 and were liquidated by the Emergency Farm Mortgage Act of 1933. Most of the JSLBs appear to have been dubious ventures from near the inception of the program.

Most investors seem to have assumed the JSLBs were government agencies—no doubt because the JSLBs were allowed to issue tax-exempt bonds clearly labeled as "instrumentalities of the Government of the United States."

The protests of the sea of investors who lost out when the joint stock land banks crashed are well documented. A most succinct such protest is set forth in a letter from W.J. Dwyer Jr., vice-president of Geo. E. Bailey & Co., Inc., to the *New York Financial Chronicle* newspaper. Dwyer states that his company "purchased securities for our own account influenced by the implied guarantys [*sic*] governing these bonds." He characterizes his company and other investors as having been "duped" by the labeling of the bonds "as instrumentalities of the United States" and concludes that the losing investors "should have been originally protected with every safeguard by the Government itself."

The government officials fielding the outcry would have nothing to do with Dwyer's argument. In a letter responding to a query from Nicholas Longworth, the speaker of the United States House of Representatives, Chester Morrill, general counsel to the secretary of the treasury, first notes dryly that Longworth's complaining constituent "very probably…is a bondholder in the Kansas City Joint Stock Land Bank, now in receivership."

After several pages of discussion of the various acts and charters involved in the debate, Morrill gets down to business:

> *Although these banks are chartered by the Farm Loan Board and function under its general supervision, they are…privately owned institutions… The Government…has not assumed any liability for the bonds of the land banks…the term "instrumentalities of the Government of the United States" relates only to the exemption from taxation of the bonds and mortgages of the Federal Land Banks and the Joint Stock Land Banks, and does not imply any liability on the part of the Government in connection with the obligation of these institutions.*[2]

Of possible interest to this narrative is the fact that the joint stock land banks charter allowed for the granting of mortgages in its headquarter state and "one contiguous state." This may have been the spark of Walter Cravens's idea to exchange foreclosed farm property in the contiguous states of Kansas and Missouri—his chartered bailiwick—for the property needed for the damming of the Osage.

Walter Price Cravens was born on April 11, 1882, in Salina Kansas. His father, Richard Price Cravens, held a law degree from the University of

Missouri and had established a successful insurance and mortgage business in Salina. Prior to going into the joint stock land bank business, Walter had worked in the family business as a partner with his father.

So it was that Walter P. Cravens was perfectly positioned to get in on the joint stock land bank business at the very beginning. According to the trial transcript of the appeal of his fraud conviction, Cravens had leveraged his partnership in his father's mortgage business to organize in Salina the Liberty Joint Stock Land Bank in 1918. (In 1925, he merged Liberty Bank with the Kansas City Joint Stock Land Bank.)[3]

Ralph Wood Street was a fairly successful lawyer, investor and property developer in Kansas City. It is likely that when he met Walter Cravens, he believed he had found the funding source for his Osage River dam—a source he had been seeking for over a dozen years. It appears a dreamer joined forces with a schemer—almost always a portentous union.

In 1924, the two men, along with Walter Eyssell (a fleeting player in this drama), incorporated the Missouri Hydro-Electric Power Company "for the purpose of maintaining and operating electric power and light plants." The ownership split is revealing: of 500 shares issued, Cravens got 498, with Street and Eyssell getting one each. Then, as now, those with the gold make the rules.

In April 1925, Cravens set up a cover corporation—Farmers Fund Inc.—described in the appeals court records thusly: "organized...to deal in bonds, mortgages and securities of all kinds, and to act generally as investment brokers." The stock issue was one thousand shares at no par value—capitalization was a little under $9,000 cash and "transfer to the company of mortgages on real estate aggregating $91,015.91." The court noted that "from which the mortgages came does not appear in the record."

Farmers Fund was the same deal share-wise as the Hydro-Electric entity: Cravens got 998 shares, Street got 1 and Alice B. Todd (Cravens's longtime employee who would also go to prison on criminal charges) got the last remaining share. These two corporate entities were clearly intended to be the vehicles used to carry out the trading of land, the construction of the dam on the Osage and possibly the development of the resulting lakefront.

So it was, according to the appeals court record, on March 10, 1925, that Walter P. Cravens "caused to be executed between the Kansas City Joint Stock Land Bank and the Missouri Hydro-Electric Power Company, an agreement whereby the land bank was to trade its foreclosed farms scattered here and there over the states of Missouri and Kansas for farms within the territory to be inundated, which farms the Hydro-Electric

Company would purchase from the land bank at an agreed value." This agreement, called the "Trading Agreement," was signed on behalf of the land bank by Cravens and on behalf of the Hydro-Electric Company by its secretary, "one Eyssell":

> *Eyssell who signed the contract as secretary owned one share in the Hydro-Electric Company, while Cravens, who signed for the land bank owned 498 shares of the 500 shares of that company…*
>
> *The Government contends that Cravens with this contract as seeming protection, started out to engineer a $30,000,000 development the success of which was at the time highly problematical.*

Indeed, the court demonstrated a flair for understatement in deploying the phrase "highly problematical."

Chapter 6

FISHING FOR A BIG FISH

In 1987, Doc Foster recalled that Ralph Street and a cohort of surveyors, engineers and real estate negotiators showed up in the north central Ozarks sometime in 1925 or 1926.

The men were offering five dollars for a three-year option on property, and they wanted to trade land for land elsewhere. After noting that nothing came of the attempt and that he had then thought the dam would never be built, Foster summed up thusly: "They was fishing for a big fish…and never did catch it." That summation of Street's mid-1920s attempt would become the generally accepted view of his and Cravens's grand scheme.

Meanwhile, back in Kansas City, Cravens continued building house of cards–style entities on the foundation of the joint stock land banks house of cards.

Although the losses from investment in JSLB bonds probably would not have been mitigated, it may be helpful to point out that until the Banking Act of 1933, there was very little in the way of regulation of the nation's financial infrastructure (with a nod to the founding of the Federal Reserve System and Woodrow Wilson's "Federal Trade Commission Act").[1]

When the 1920s federal government finally sent examiners to determine the extent of Cravens's fraudulent use of his land bank funds and assets—a dramatic raid on the KCJSLB offices—the examiners were individuals appointed by the Farm Loan Board along with Secret Service agents under the supervision of the office of the secretary of the treasury.

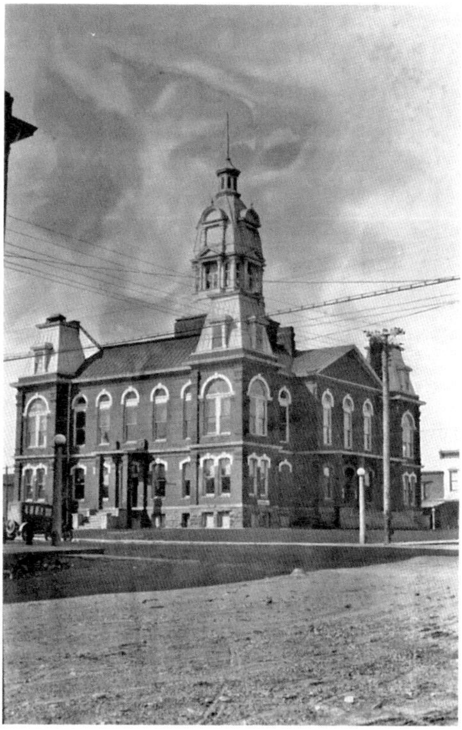

The Morgan County Courthouse, very majestic with its tall dome, was the area gathering place for community events. *Courtesy of Morgan County Historical Society.*

Court records indicate Cravens had fraudulently transferred substantial funds from the land bank to his cover corporations and had apparently at one point used a kind of check-kiting scheme to try to conceal some of the criminal activity. Additionally, he may have engaged in some pretty spectacular stock manipulation. He was actively abetted by his secretary, Alice Todd.[2] The misappropriated funds had been used for surveying and mapping in the proposed dam area, as well as to secure some of the options and transactions that were part of the land trading scheme.

Cravens's indictment on criminal fraud and misappropriation charges came in 1927. He was convicted and went through the appeals process—which he lost.

Except for being included in the initial indictment, Ralph W. Street escaped the court's attention, probably because he clearly was not involved in the fraudulent activity and may not have had even an inkling of what was going on back in Kansas City while he was out trudging the Ozarks. Walter Eyssell was not subject to indictment—he had died in 1926.

It is impossible to know what Cravens was thinking when he stepped out on the dam undertaking. Cravens would maintain that if the government hadn't interfered, he would have gotten the dam built and all the money from the KCJSLB would have been returned.

It is equally difficult to discern what motivated Street. Ozarks legend has it that he was a principal in brokering the deal with Union Electric (UE) to take over the failed dam project and that he used money gotten as his part of the UE buyout to pay off the debts of the Cravens cover companies.

By then, though, other parties were involved, and with UE's resources, the "big fish" that Cravens and Street had been fishing for could indeed be hooked. And the pair had laid enough groundwork on the project to prove its feasibility and accelerate its final execution. In fact, they somehow had purchased or secured quite a number of land deals, the disposition of which would then fall to the receiver in the KCJSLB bankruptcy.

As Cravens was dispatched to prison, Street took a job with Union Electric. He became a major player in the company's community liaison, pacification and mollification operations, and he seems to have had a good grasp on what was needed in that regard by then.

Here is a report from the March 5, 1931 *Versailles Statesman*:

> *In a mass meeting held in the courthouse at Versailles last summer looking to a satisfactory adjustment and settlement to both parties concerned in county roads and bridge matters, R.W. Street of the land and development division of the Union Electric Light and Power Co. promised the assembled citizens that the company would pay the salary of a competent engineer to go over that part of the county which would be damaged by the lake formed by the Bagnell Dam and that the company would be willing to settle upon the facts and figures found by this engineer.*

In some accounts, this is where Street and Cravens exit the Osage Project saga. But there is more to their venture, and that will be explored later in this narrative.

Street passed away at the age of seventy. His obituary, in the May 16, 1953 *Kansas City Times*, noted that he "was credited with the conception of Bagnell Dam, which resulted in the Lake of the Ozarks."

CHAPTER 7

HOMESTEAD AND SQUAT

Abraham Lincoln signed the Homestead Act into law in the middle years of the Civil War. It provided that any person over twenty-one years of age or who was the head of the family and who had not taken up arms against the United States was entitled to claim 160 acres of land (a "Lot" or a "Quarter of a Section") if one could prove they had lived on and cultivated said "Lot" for a period of five years.

There was never a "forty acres and a mule" federal act. That post–Civil War field order proposal was never enacted.

Squatters rights, however, were taken very seriously in the Ozark population that Street would be dealing with in the great evacuation the dam project required.

The underlying tenet of the squat—that is to say the use and care of the land—was highly honored even when ownership was not in issue. It is said that a tenant farmer or renter would seldom be evicted by an Ozarks sheriff during the growing season if he had even one crop still in the field. Another issue, noted by Gerard Schultz, was that the eviction of a squatter by a legal claimant was frowned upon in most parts of the Ozarks, and that claimant often was soon discovered shot to death on some lonesome glade or forested byway.

Some of the interior Ozarks land, mountainous and untillable, no doubt would have been acquired under the "Graduation Act of 1854." Schultz wrote:

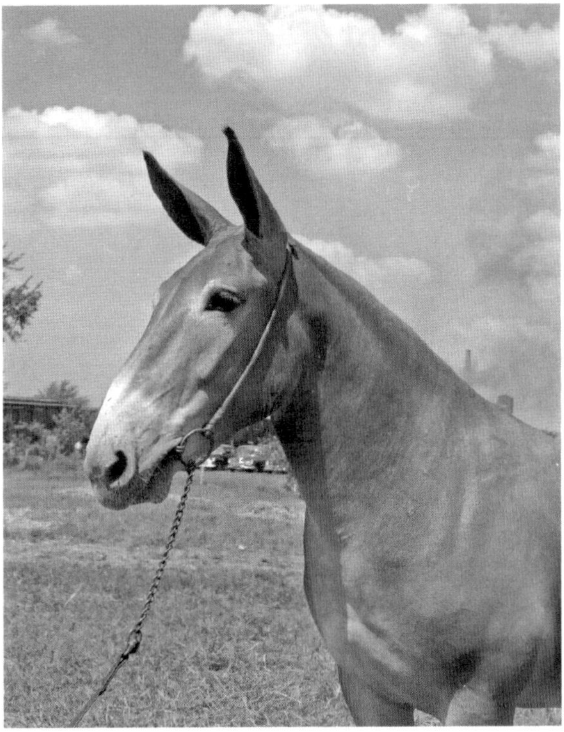

Right: The Missouri mule is a state icon and a very reliable part of the Ozark way of life. *Courtesy of Missouri State Capitol Commission, Missouri State Archives.*

Below: This Missouri mule team represents the native Ozarker's most important possession. Quite often, the mules are worked as a team. *Courtesy of Missouri State Capitol Commission, Missouri State Archives.*

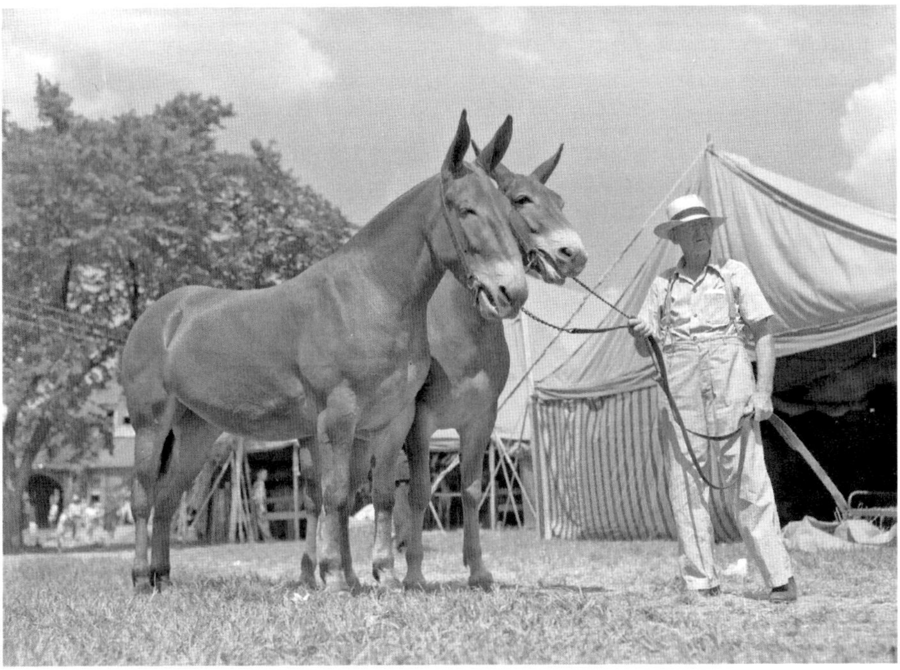

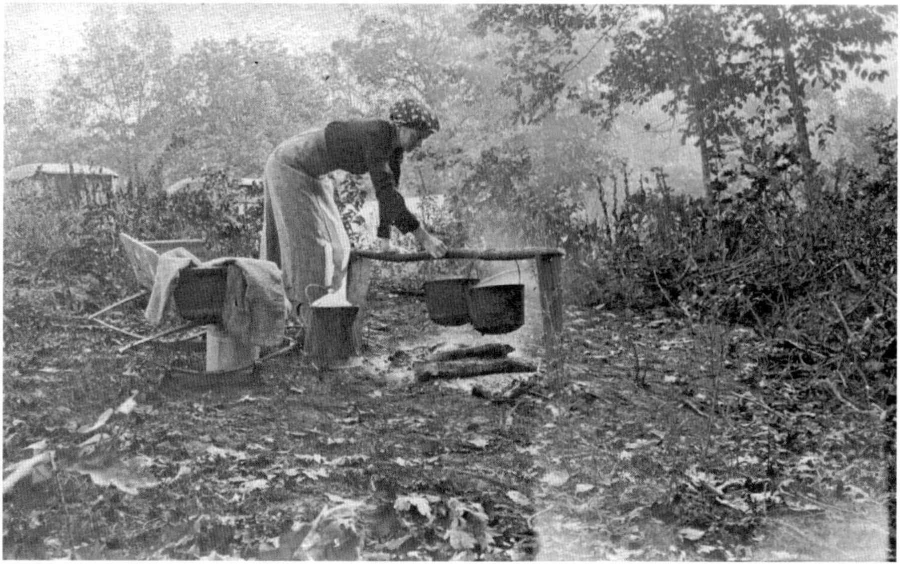

This early twentieth-century photo of a woman making lye soap demonstrates a housewife's specific chore and is an example of the division of labor. *Courtesy of Missouri State Capitol Commission, Missouri State Archives.*

> *The Graduation Act…reduced the price of slow selling lands, by progressive stages, to a merely nominal sum. The price schedule was based on intervals that the land remained unsold, with the final price of twelve and one half cents per acre at 30 years. Thus 40 acres could be purchased for five dollars at that point. The total acreage that could be purchased under the Act was capped at 320 acres.*[1]

Land platting was blurred further by the "free range" nature of the regions animal husbandry and such matters as communal hunting and fishing understandings that were common in parts of the interior Ozarks until the mid-twentieth century.

Well into the twentieth century, the concept of "private" property rights was coexistent with that of free range. In the 1920s population with which Ralph Street and Union Electric dealt, however, many had obtained their properties through sweat and tears or for hard-earned cash money under the original Homestead, Preemption or Graduation Acts.[2] The mid-1920s were little more than six decades distant from the passage of the Homestead Act, a couple or so generations past.

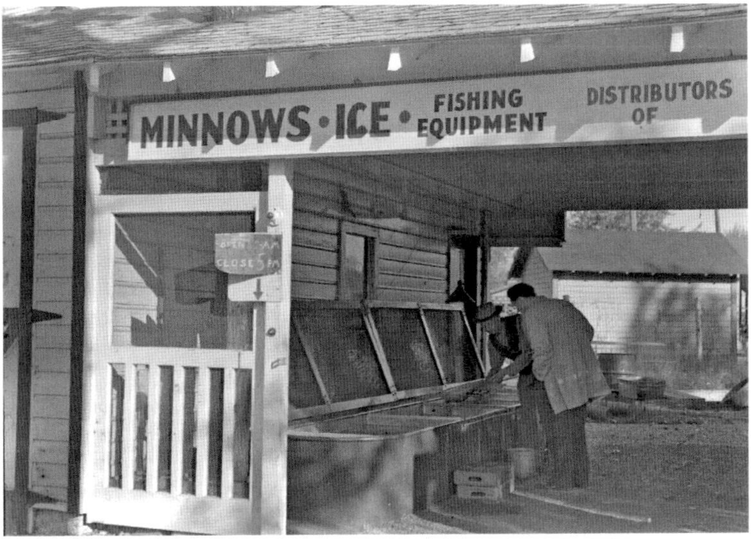

This early lake-area 1950s-era bait and tackle store provided everything a fisherman needed for an enjoyable day on the water. *Courtesy of Missouri State Capitol Commission, Missouri State Archives.*

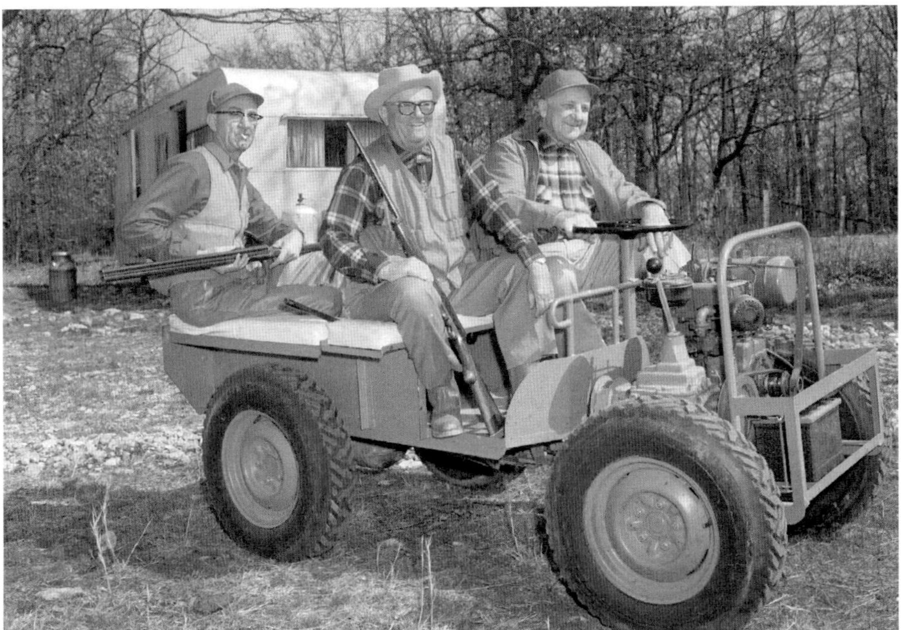

The "good ol' boys" hunting with their homemade ATV, trailer and a milk can full of water—everything you need for a hunt! *Courtesy of Missouri State Capitol Commission, Missouri State Archives.*

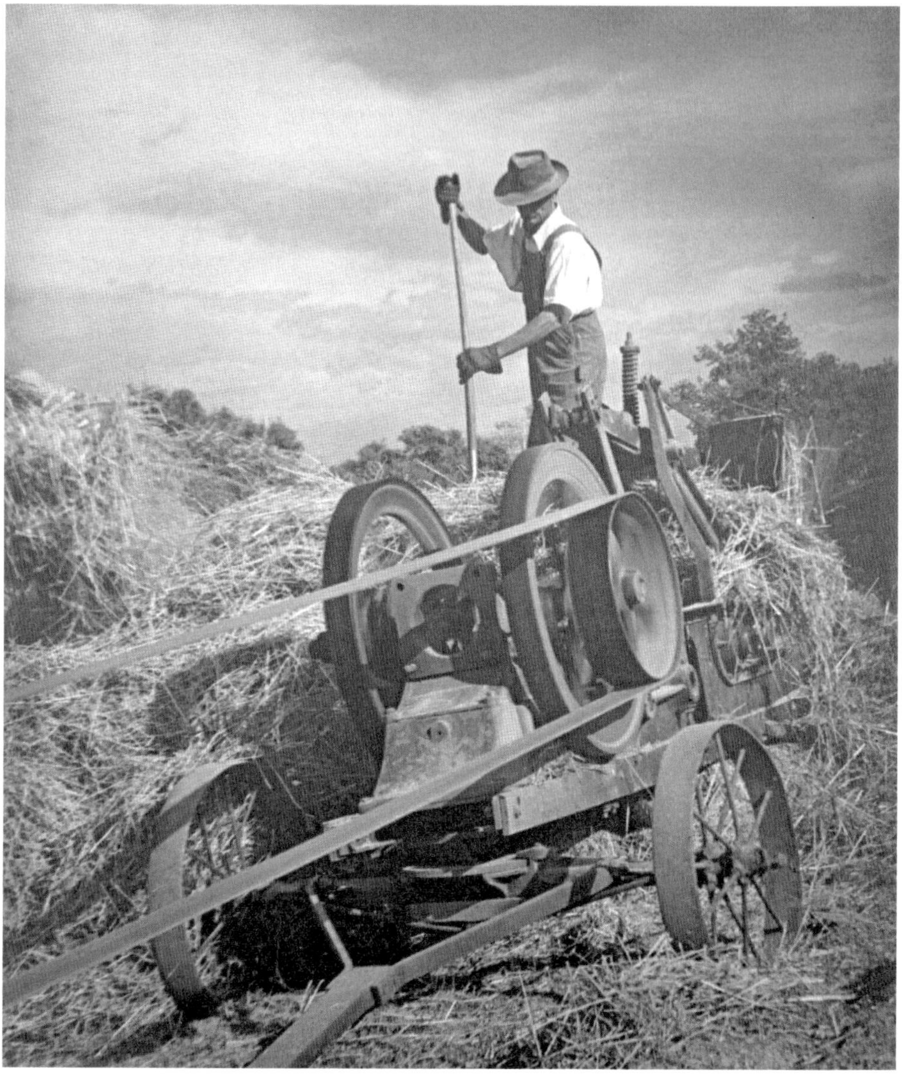

Early farming machines were not mobile. This stationary hay baler required the cut hay and straw to be delivered to the machine, which was common in the early 1900s. *Courtesy of Missouri State Capitol Commission, Missouri State Archives.*

The old-timers of the region, however, were in agreement that the deals Street and UE struck with most of the affected landowners were, in the final analysis, fair. This was particularly so with bottomland acreage that had been periodically enriched by river flood silt and thus had considerable commercial value.

Lee Mace, who will figure prominently further along in this narrative, said it was those who did not own land—the renters and share tenants—who suffered most perilously in the mass relocation.

Victoria Pope Hubbell documented the local sentiment:

> *Fifty years later Doc Foster recalled the reaction of local residents. "You take a young man, he can adjust. But you take a man sixty or sixty-five years old and put everything in his vest pocket and start him up the hill on foot and his probability of getting started again wasn't too good. He'd left everything he had behind him."*

Speaking further to the point Lee Mace had made, Victoria Hubbell wrote:

> *Ralph McDowell was a tenant farmer using the land under the Grand Glaize Bridge in the last years before the Dam. Because he did not own the land where he raised corn, he did not receive monetary compensation for the loss of his livelihood. His horse drawn farm equipment was suddenly as useless as his knowledge of riverbottom farming. When asked "What did you do then?" he simply replied, "I walked to Linn Creek and got a job."*

Those who would not sell were flushed out through eminent domain, even though at the time the doctrine was not supposedly interpreted as a tool for private gain.

It may be worth noting that when the majority of justices of the U.S. Supreme Court voted to "privatize" eminent domain during the early years of the twenty-first century, it was but one more sign the pre-Depression laissez faire politics had returned—possibly one of the more notable such signals since the repeal of the protections of the 1933 Banking Act in the late 1990s.[3]

However uprooted, the Ozarkers may have found entertainment in one of the first of the Lake of the Ozarks turf wars—a kind of soap-opera scenario involving serious money.

In the early twentieth century, a wealthy business owner from Kansas City, Robert McClure Snyder Sr., decided to build a "castle" for his family's personal benefit on a spectacular cliff-top spread overlooking five thousand acres of pristine Ozarks on the Niangua River. The property had been dubbed "Ha Ha Tonka"—said to translate from the local Native American tongue as "land of laughing waters" (good to learn that the aboriginals engaged in occasional onomatopoeic poetics).

This was in the days of extravagant mansion construction by the barons of commerce and industry. Anyone who has toured the manses of Newport, Rhode Island, will have some sense of what may have been Snyder's inspiration for his castle. The project commenced in 1905, but then Snyder Sr. was killed in 1906 in an automobile accident in Kansas City.

The Snyder family pressed on with the plans for their grand castle in the Ozarks, spending a reported half million dollars to finally complete the project in 1922. But the surviving Snyders couldn't afford to keep up the extravagant castle and grounds.

The Snyder heirs got the idea that they should sell the pile to the state of Missouri for use as a resort and state park. The state viewed the offer with indifference. The transaction did transpire decades later in 1978—too late to do the Snyders any good.

But in 1931, in an ex post facto notice, Union Electric gave the Snyder heirs the news that the Lake of the Ozarks, already in full flood, would inundate a portion of their castle property. But UE would be happy to pay them $143,000 for the expropriation.

The Snyders did not accept the deal and sued for $1.3 million. But what it all boiled down to was wealthy city folks—Kansas City's Snyders and Louis Egan (president of St. Louis–based UE)—engaging in expensive litigation over land and power in the Ozarks, foreshadowing aspects of the urbanized cultural overlay of the region in the decades to come.[4]

Chapter 8

Witness Trees and Peep Sights

Dexter Slagle came to the Lake of the Ozarks as a twenty-four-year-old surveyor in 1953. He would pass the next forty-five years mapping much of the region's property. In his first assignment, he platted the area on the east side of the Gravois arm of the lake, known as Golden Beach.

"Thirteen hundred lots," he recalled. "It took over a year—not working on it all the time though. Each lakefront lot had 50 to 75 feet of shoreline."

With original 1931 UE plat maps of the entire Lake of the Ozarks on the table before him, Slagle reviewed how land is surveyed and platted and the methods of doing so in olden days.

The plat maps are fairly straightforward. "Township lines" and "range lines" intersect rows of neatly leaning blocks, each representing a square mile or "a section." Slagle notes that the blocks are periodically elongated because every thirty-six miles, the curvature of the earth must be accounted for and represented.[1]

One of the challenges of surveying in the early days was that some of the land had been acquired through squatters rights.

"Those [squatter] surveys are called 'New Madrid surveys,'" Slagle said. "In 1811 and 1812, there were earthquakes in the Boot Heel along the New Madrid Fault. And a number of people moved out of the area for good."

The New Madrid Fault is a seam between the platelets of the earth where they intersect at midcontinent North America. The New Madrid Earthquakes are seared as one in national memory—the largest ever such event in recorded American history.[2]

"A good number of [these squatters] moved to Howard County, where Fayette is now," Slagle said, "and claimed new homes by squatters rights. When you do squatters rights ownership, you don't survey, you just mark off your claim and it is identified by a 'New Madrid' number on a plat recorded in the courthouse. That is why the entire older part of Fayette is shaped in a kind of northwestern-leaning rectangle. That area was all done with New Madrid surveys," which is to say they were plat mapped after the fact of ownership had already been established.

Land claimed through the Homestead or Graduation Acts was surveyed in some manner. In the early days of American survey practice, though, accuracy was not always achieved, and the methods of marking boundaries often involved the use of trees, called "witness trees."

The term is near self-explanatory: the surveyor stamped a brand into usually two trees to be used in recording and identifying (or resetting lost) section and quarter section markers—pacing off from "corner marker" stones or stakes to the witness trees provided a means of approximating accuracy in the platting. This type of survey methodology is known as "metes and bounds"—localized measurement and boundaries.

Slagle had a collection of surveyor memorabilia, including two marked witness tree sections and a Colonial-period surveyor's compass with "peep sights"—aligned notches to guide the eye. Slagle noted that the antique had a sixty-six-foot chain (an English measurement), which was used in measuring land until the early 1900s, when a one-hundred-foot steel tape—the American standard—was introduced.

In more modern times, boundaries were marked with metal pins or pipes, and the surveyor's instruments had telescopes for much more accuracy than in the old days.

Dexter Slagle, in an interview, described the evolution of his survey equipment:

> *In 1983, I bought a new type of surveyor's transit. It shot a laser beam from the transit to a glass reflector on a pole, which gave a level measurement up to a mile. This made surveying much more accurate and a lot less time consuming. About ten years later, GPS came into use. It could read angles and measurements over great distances and did not have to be line of sight. This made land surveying even more accurate and took even less time to complete a job and only requires two men on a survey team instead of three.*

When attention was turned to the 1931 Union Electric plat maps, the story of the creation of the Lake of the Ozarks took a critical turn. The majority portion of the land bordering or in what is now the lake bed was, according to the plat maps, by then owned by the Kansas City Joint Stock Land Bank. In fact, most of the land needed for flooding the section of the reservoir abutting Bagnell Dam had been acquired by the Kansas City JSLB when the plat maps were created, according to the UE 1931 plat map numbered 5.

Some accounts of the creation of the Lake of the Ozarks present Craven and Street's scheme as a complete failure, saying that the "big fish" they were after was never caught. That they did not see the effort through as originally conceived is correct, but they came closer than is generally credited.

Apparently, Street and his land acquisition crews ranged the entire length of the stretch of Osage River to be flooded, from far up in Benton County to the Bagnell area where the dam was to be constructed. They appear to have successfully managed to make numerous land deals with the locals.

This should not have been too unexpected, since most of the land to be submerged by the new lake was steeply hilled, rocky and essentially worthless in terms of commercial farming or other use. The farmland being traded was located down-land and no doubt was at least somewhat arable.

A visit to the Morgan County Recorder of Deeds office revealed that the plan to use cover corporations was indeed put into effect. There in the 1927 "Reverse Abstract and Index to Deeds," handwritten entries in a huge, heavy, age-worn volume reveal row upon row of deed and affidavit transfers of property to the Kansas City Joint Stock Land Bank from Farmers Fund, Inc. The consideration in the deals was always "One Dollar and Other Good and Valuable Considerations." The notarized signature was that of Walter Cravens, as president of Farmers Fund, Inc. The witness was A.B. Todd—Alice, the loyal secretary.

It seems the original scheme was to have Farmers Fund, Inc., act as cover in the purchasing and trading aspect and then transfer the procured land to the Missouri Hydro-Electric Power Company (another of Cravens's cover or "straw" entities). But apparently Cravens lost patience or found some flaw with that process and caused the land to remain titled to Kansas City JSLB—only one or two of the purchases were transferred to the power company—making no further attempt to cover his tracks.

So Cravens controlled the entity—Farmers Fund, Inc.—that made the land deals and also the entity to which the land was ultimately transferred, the Kansas City JSLB. And which hat he wore depended on where he was in the transaction.[3]

It has been said that Cravens was himself, at the end, attempting to broker a deal that would have enabled the completion of his dam scheme. Had that been the case and had he escaped criminal prosecution, Walter P. Cravens would certainly be now a name to reckon with in the history of American business—if no other reason than for sheer audacity alone.

Chapter 9

The Lilac Memory

(KVL)

The construction of the dam was started in 1929 by the Union Electric Company of St. Louis, Missouri, for an electrical power supply plant. The heavy construction was carried on from 1929 until early 1931, when the dam was completed. According to Union Electric officials, at the peak employment period, there were between three thousand and five thousand men employed in the building of the dam.

The preliminary studies included gathering data for a location of the dam and a survey to determine what land would be flooded by the lake. Before the construction started, there was also the building of a construction camp for the work crews in the area.

At the time the dam was built, it created what was thought to be the largest inland man-made lake in the world. To construct the dam, a railroad right-of-way had to be built to haul the materials to the site. The maximum number of men employed at one time was 4,634, the average being 3,000 men. The total number of different employees hired was about 20,500. A thesis on the subject states:

> *The construction on the dam was around-the-clock work from the beginning, without even closing down in the winter months, when the pouring of concrete was begun it did not stop until the dam was completed, since they could not pour concrete on top of concrete that had already set.*

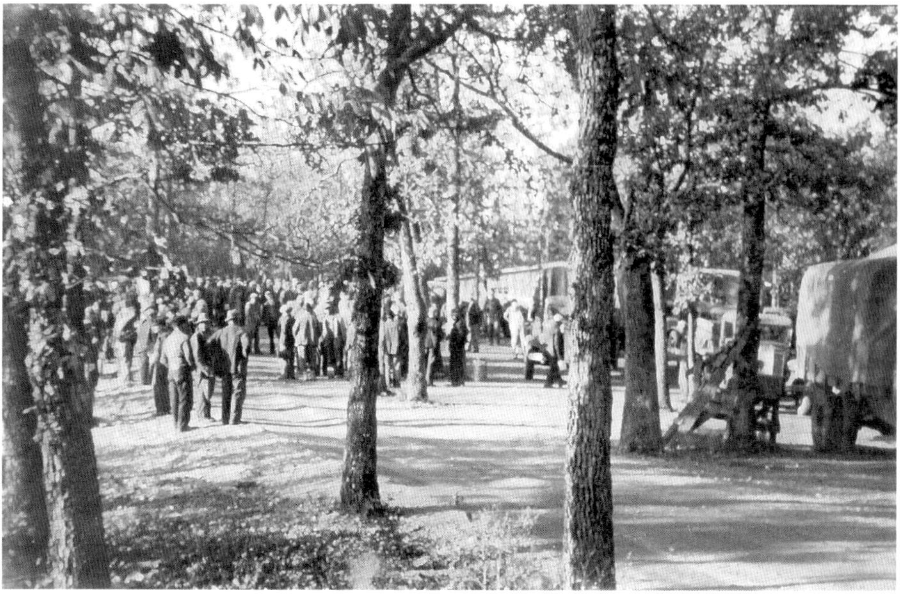

The 1930s federal New Deal program helped fund State Park #1 construction. This provided another great Depression-era employment opportunity soon after the dam was completed. *Courtesy of Miller County Missouri Historical Society.*

In 1987, Camden County's Doc Foster would recall average pay for common labor on the dam of about thirty-five cents an hour. He also noted that the UE managers and the engineers and personnel from the East Coast–based engineering firm Stone & Webster, which planned and oversaw the construction, were paid considerably more.

The principal benefit to the locals, Foster noted, was that there "was no Depression here." Ernest McNeil, who was Doc's first cousin and best second in the tales both men liked to spin, said that at the time his family had moved back to the Oklahoma Dust Bowl and there had been for sure a Great Depression going on out there.

This is one of the first things many interior Ozarkers will bring up on the subject of the lake, and they use the same phrase: "There was no Depression here." The information seems to have been passed generationally since some informants were too young to have experienced the Great Depression.

Albert Gray "Al" Elam of Camden County recalled that Union Electric accomplished procurement of land for the Osage Project in three ways: by outright purchase, by the purchase of easements (covenants for the use of property for shoreline and inundation) and by condemnation (forced sale through court-ordered right of eminent domain).

In Camden County, the acquisition of land was complicated further by the fact that the county courthouse in Old Linn Creek had burned to the ground in 1902, with all records gone to ashes. This may be one reason Union Electric routinely litigated to assure "quiet title" even in cases where there was little likelihood of contest. According to Al Elam, no matter how the land was acquired, title litigation was standard policy with UE—which is to say the company routinely petitioned to validate by court order the title to the property being acquired.

Dexter Slagle pointed out notations on the 1931 UE plat maps that documented that land purchased outright was measured from 662 feet above sea level. Easements were purchased at 660 feet above sea level and land acquired through condemnation at a 665-foot boundary.

These boundaries were benchmarked from mean sea level (MSL) as measured at Biloxi, Mississippi. This type of boundary is what is called a "contour boundary"—continuous, non-local measurement as opposed to "metes and bounds" or localized measurement. Most of the lake shoreline was established with contour boundary survey.

Another important measurement of the lake, as noted by Al Elam, was its depth of 630 feet, below which would not create enough water pressure

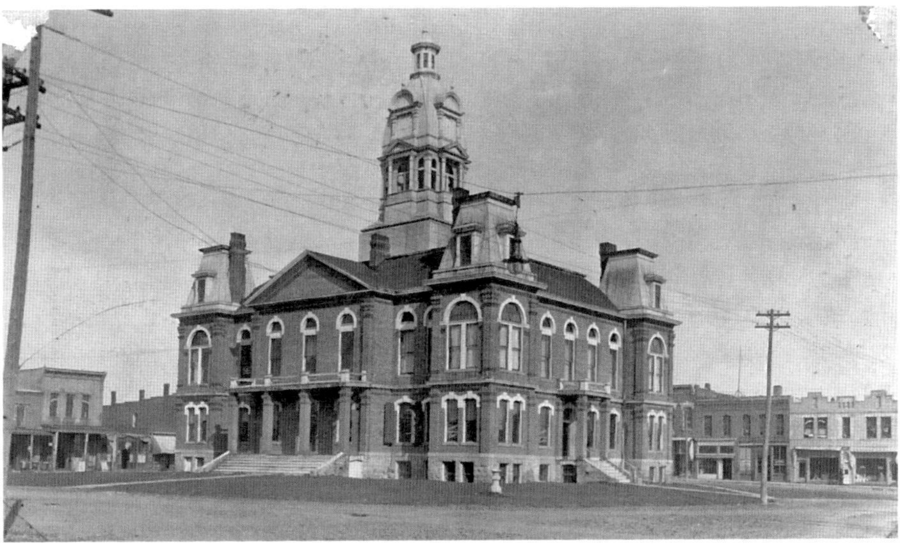

Southside view of Morgan County Courthouse in Versailles. *Courtesy of Morgan County Historical Society.*

to run the turbines. (T. Victor Jeffries wrote that UE had cleared the land between 628 feet and 660 feet above MSL "of all timber and houses.") The lake boundaries would become a considerable controversy some eight decades after the lake crested.

In accounts of the genesis of the Lake of the Ozarks, there is usually a mention of the necessity of the relocation of graves. In cultural context, the removal and reinterment of thousands of ancestral remains is perhaps the starkest symbol of the casually wrought destruction of nature and the social disruption brought about by the impoundment of the Osage.

In the Ozarks of those days, the tradition of burial with the footing facing east would have been strictly adhered to. This practice is so that on Resurrection Morning—"when the trumpet of the Lord shall sound and time shall be no more and the morning breaks eternal bright and fair"—the patiently slumbering dead will rise up to behold immediately the glory of that preternatural sunrise.

Bill Williams, who with his wife and fellow historian, Dorothy, had numbered and named the inhabitants of the cemeteries of Morgan County, recalled hearing Union Electric employed a crew of eighty men to accomplish the relocation of as many graves as could be discovered in the districts of inundation.

The Williamses consulted their cemetery records to enable the tracking of a sample of those transported from their original resting place to another. They believed odds were certain that the footings of the relocation graves would face the culturally correct direction, since most were removed to existing church plots. Their records of the re-interred came directly from the source, UE original documents archived in the catacomb of offices that is encased in the concrete core of Bagnell Dam.

The cemetery visited is not far from Rocky Mount, a small town nestled in the interior Ozarks proximate to the Morgan-Miller County line, not far from Bagnell Dam. On a humid overcast August noon at the church cemetery, a half dozen evenly spaced gunshots were fired nearby—somewhere in the surrounding woods—then silence. A Confederate battle flag presided limply over the mysterious salute from atop the farmstead flagpole directly across the two-lane paved but shoulder-less county highway fronting the church grounds.

The church's burial realm is divided in three, labeled "Original," "Section One" and "Section Two" on the meticulous cemetery cartography created by the Williamses. All of the great dam flood graves are at the very rear of the cemetery, in the Original section, hard by the narrow highway. The occasional passing motor vehicle punctuated the quiet of the backcountry summer day.

The footings of the graves all pointed the direction of the sun's rise.

There was a sense of unsettling solemnity about the scene—a haunting poignancy hovered in the several rows of three-by-five metal placards rising a few inches above the grass on slender steel pins. Only one of the placard-marked graves was decorated, with a single white artificial flower. The bright faux flower rested gently, like a whispered prayer, on the anonymous grave site.

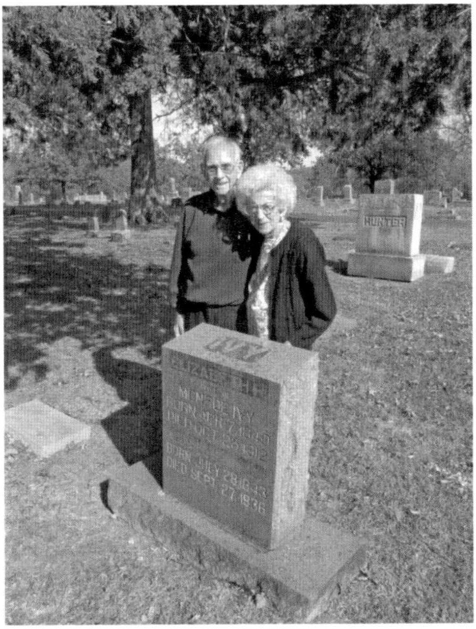

Bill and Dorothy Williams are well-known Morgan County historians. Their major accomplishments included identification of all graves in Morgan County. This includes the graves relocated beyond the high water mark of the Lake of the Ozarks. Bill and Dorothy are shown standing next to the grave marker of General Monroe Ivy. *Author's private collection (DWP).*

Bill Williams explained that if a grave to be removed to make way for the lake flood had a formal marker or stone, that memorial would have been moved with the remains. If not, the new grave site was marked only with a numbered metal placard such as those that now populate that section of consecrated earth at the Rocky Mount Church.

The cultural trauma manifest in the forced transport of the Ozark graves to plots where both the person and place of the departed are obscured is more profound than might immediately emerge. The sense of place and identity is powerful with Ozarkers, perhaps much more so than with more urban, mobile populations of other regions.

An Ozarker's name often connects specifically to previous generations as an intense identity and place marker. In rural Ozark towns for example, addresses—regardless of street and number designation—are often known by the name of a family or a person most commonly associated with the place. Sometimes even after the building is gone, the traditional address remains: "where the Curtis house was."

Ozarker names can signify—in addition to personal identity—an encompassing community connection. Bill Williams, for example, was known in his youth as "Billy Woodin"—William Woodin Williams being his full name. But the sobriquet—usually spoken as one name, *Billywoodin*—connected his lineage specifically with Morgan County's first (long remembered and revered) female doctor, his grandmother Elsie Woodin.[1]

As further example of the enduring community markers of Ozarker names, James Franklin Sr., the Osage Beach banker introduced in the 1987 video, was the grandson of "Swede Charlie" Anderson. Franklin's brother Clarence L. was said to have been nicknamed "Swede"—again a means of affixing his identity in the culture.

Chapter 10

THE MYSTERY OF THE LAKE

Thus there became Bagnell Dam and its lake. Here is a description by the lake's preeminent historian and pictorial preservationist H. Dwight Weaver of the very first weekend at the Lake of the Ozarks as viewed from the nearby town of Eldon:

> *The character and friendly nature of the local people is best illustrated by what occurred on May 30, 1931, when the dam was officially opened for traffic…*
>
> *"By Saturday night of that Memorial Weekend," a newspaper account related, "visitors had flocked to Eldon on their way to the dam and took residents by surprise. By 8 p.m., hotels were full in the city, and 126 people had called for rooms at the James House…* [which was] *more than could be accommodated."*
>
> *Hotel managers and personnel of service stations, cafes and other business places called citizens of the city and many took the tourists into their homes overnight, providing breakfast the next morning.*

The *Kansas City Star* newspaper sent a reporter and a photographer to witness the opening of Bagnell Dam. The result was a lengthy article datelined "Bagnell Dam, Mo. May 30," bylined "By a member of the Star's Staff" and headlined "Exploring Reaches of the Southwest's Greatest Lake."[1] The report subtitle read: "A Motor Boat Trip on the Spreading Waters Above the Bagnell Dam Discloses Hundreds of Miles of Newly Formed Shore Lines of Great Scenic Beauty, Islands That Have Not Been

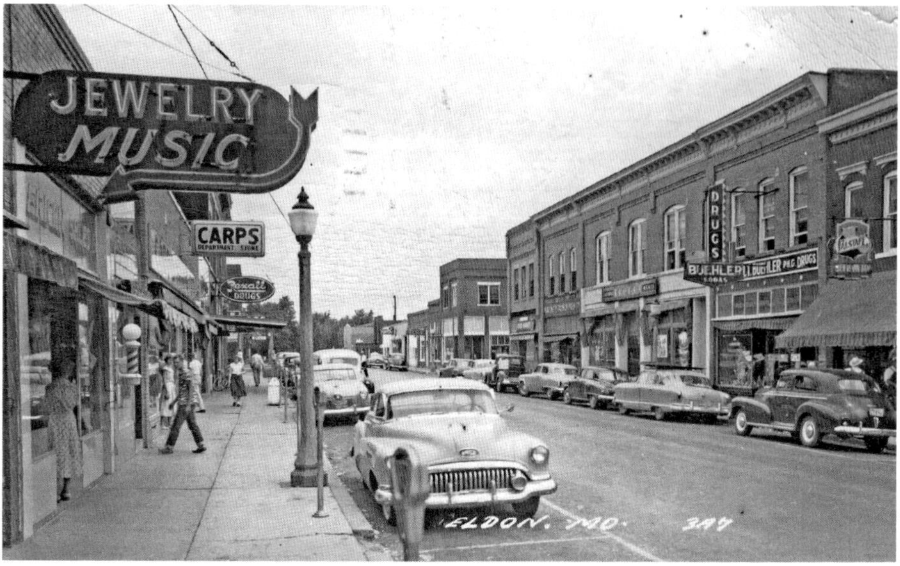

An early 1950s view of downtown Eldon, looking north from the area of the Missouri Pacific Depot. Note the variety of recognizable businesses and vehicles. *Courtesy of Miller County Missouri Historical Society.*

Named and Countless Sites for Summer Homes—Snags and Floating Logs Make Navigation Hazardous on the Upper End Now."[2]

This latter statement about snags and logs is part of the lake's oral history as well. Al Elam noted that forty-foot sycamore fragments and the like sometimes shot to the surface in the early days of the lake, having been loosed by rust or rot from the chains with which UE personnel had secured piles of cleared timber in the lakebed before the flood.

For several years after the creation of the lake, UE had boat crews out hauling these remnants of the destruction of nature to the lakeshore, where they would dry and burn the dangerous detritus.

The *Star* reporter included directions to the lake from Kansas City "over surfaced roads all the way." The route was "Highway 50, through Warrensburg and Sedalia to Tipton and south from there through Versailles to Gravois." (Note the care with description—"surfaced roads" rather than "paved," which would have been inaccurate.)

If a visit to the dam was desired, the recommended route was from Versailles to Eldon "and thence south to Bagnell and the dam."

Although some tourist camp and cabin operations opened shortly after the creation of the lake, it is not clear how profitable they were. These were generally live-in family businesses, catering to fishing and boating folk and offering few amenities. Some had romantic names like "Silver Moon," while others reflected pride of ownership: "Washburn's Point." Many opted for descriptive lure: "Beauty View" and "Holiday House."

While photographs of these early resorts usually include people swimming or boating, there does not seem to have been much in the way of marketing to any cities of the region, and indeed, the lack of amenities would have limited the market.

The general opinion in the Lake of the Ozarks oral history is that the Depression and the Second World War delayed any extensive development of the lake front. The fact is, too, that Union Electric—perhaps operating in unfamiliar territory as real estate developers—could find few buyers for its lakefront properties. Al Elam, who came to the lake in 1936 and eventually went to work for the UE land development company, remembered that lake property was offered at that time at one dollar per waterfront foot—and that there were few takers.[3]

(KVL) But what neither the media nor the tourists nor the locals could know as the 1931 waters rose to full crest at Bagnell Dam was that the life of the

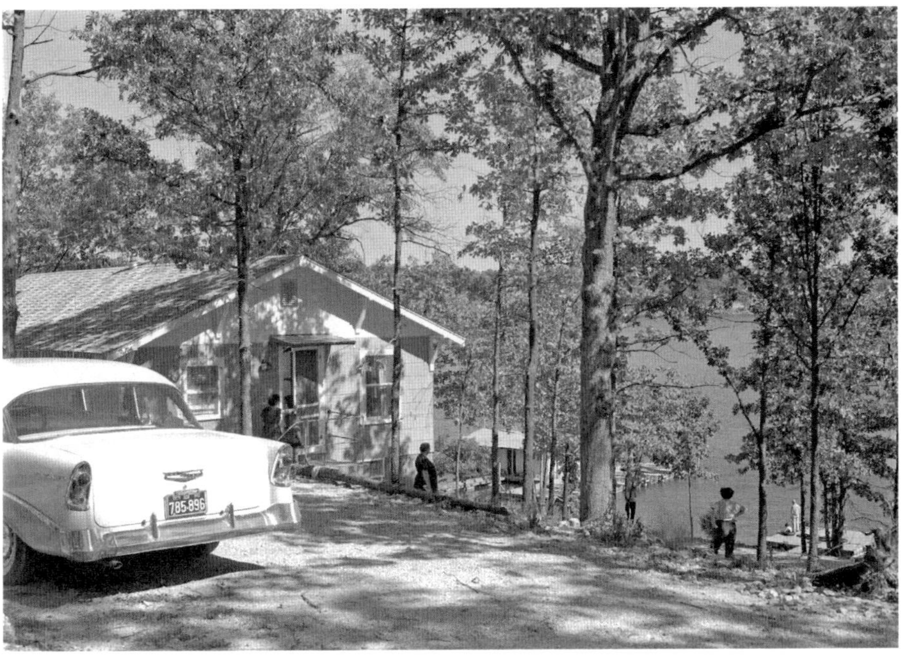

An example of a 1950s lakeside rental cabin. This was the standard for the time. *Courtesy of Miller County Missouri Historical Society.*

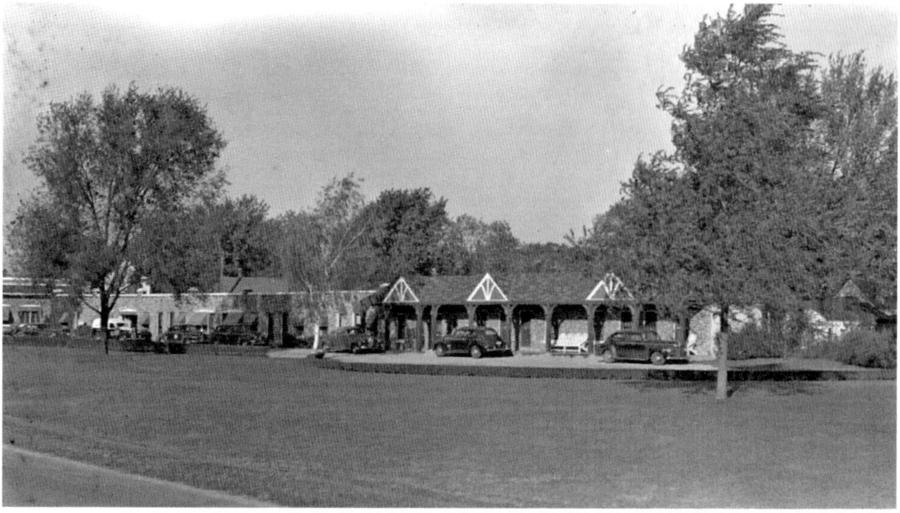

The travel courts were the first motel-style overnight tourist facilities. Travel court owner built small cabins close together, usually not connected, and rented these to their visitors. The owners preferred multiple-day or weekly rentals. This style of lodging facilities was very popular after World War II and into the 1960s. It is very similar to facilities seen on the famous Route 66 corridor across the United States. *Courtesy of Missouri State Capitol Commission, Missouri State Archives.*

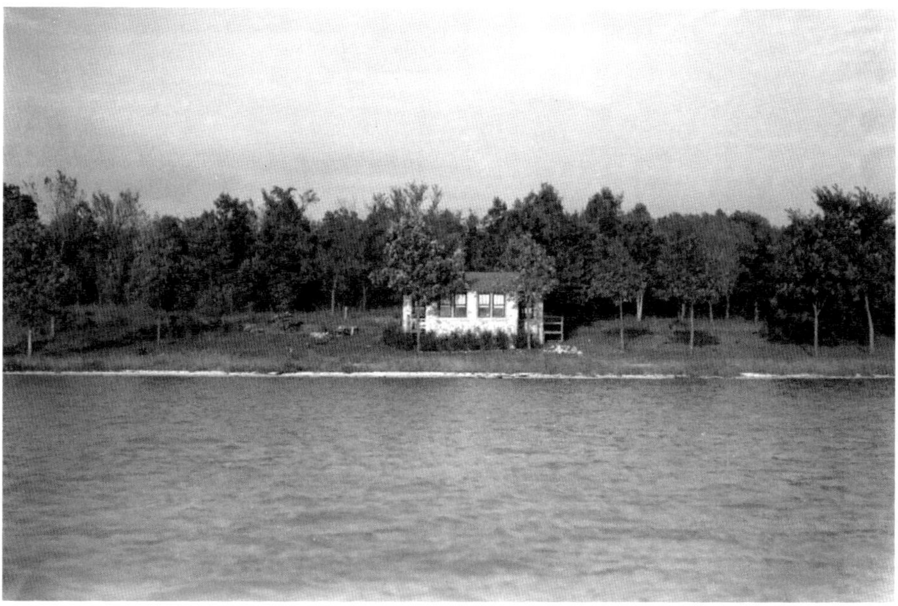

Some people liked the lake so much they chose to buy their own lot(s) and build their own cabin. This single-lot cabin is representative of an early owner cabin. *Courtesy of Missouri State Capitol Commission, Missouri State Archives.*

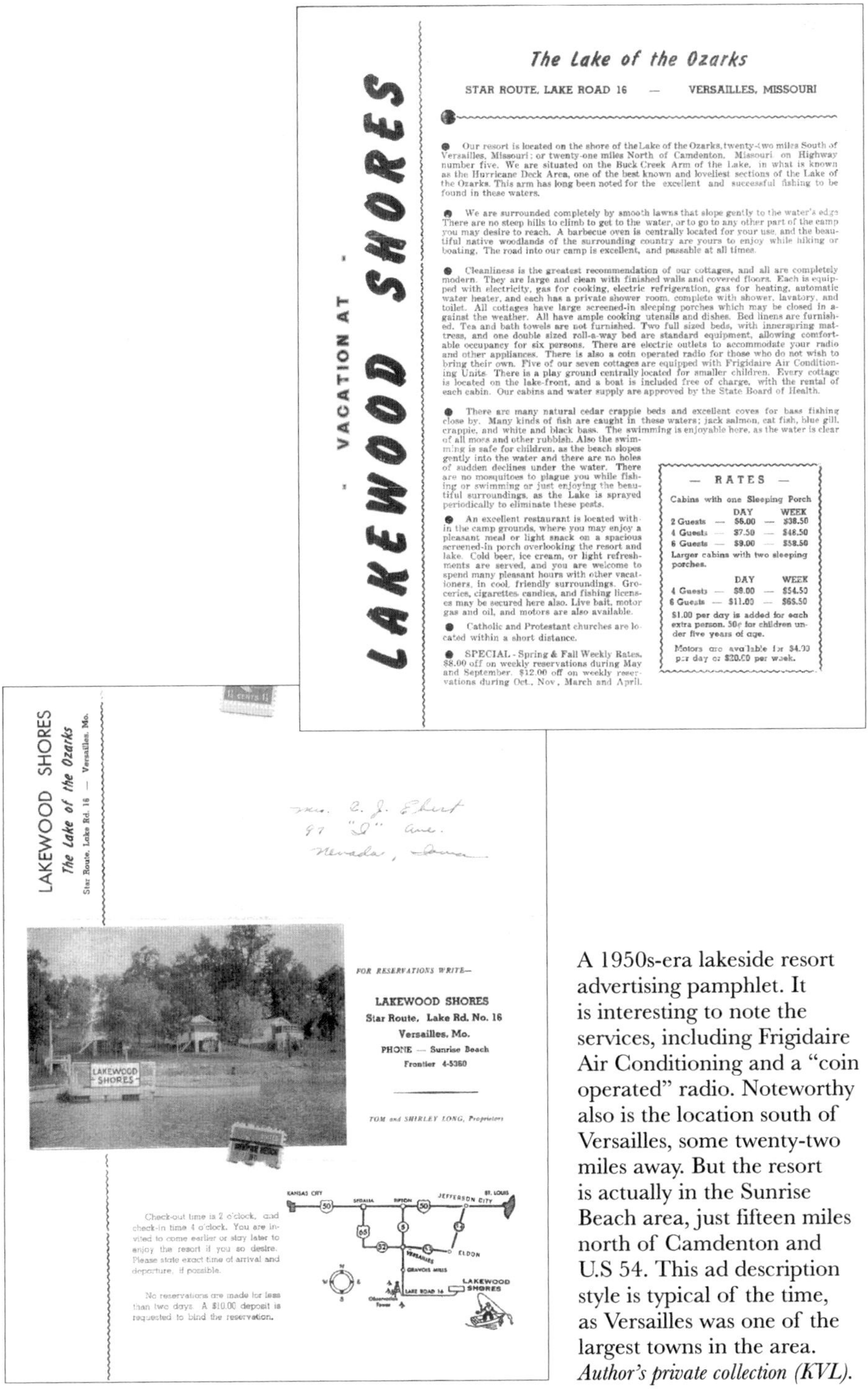

VACATION AT

LAKEWOOD SHORES

The Lake of the Ozarks

STAR ROUTE, LAKE ROAD 16 — VERSAILLES, MISSOURI

● Our resort is located on the shore of the Lake of the Ozarks, twenty-two miles South of Versailles, Missouri; or twenty-one miles North of Camdenton, Missouri on Highway number five. We are situated on the Buck Creek Arm of the Lake, in what is known as the Hurricane Deck Area, one of the best known and loveliest sections of the Lake of the Ozarks. This arm has long been noted for the excellent and successful fishing to be found in these waters.

● We are surrounded completely by smooth lawns that slope gently to the water's edge There are no steep hills to climb to get to the water, or to go to any other part of the camp you may desire to reach. A barbecue oven is centrally located for your use, and the beautiful native woodlands of the surrounding country are yours to enjoy while hiking or boating. The road into our camp is excellent, and passable at all times.

● Cleanliness is the greatest recommendation of our cottages, and all are completely modern. They are large and clean with finished walls and covered floors. Each is equipped with electricity, gas for cooking, electric refrigeration, gas for heating, automatic water heater, and each has a private shower room, complete with shower, lavatory, and toilet. All cottages have large screened-in sleeping porches which may be closed in against the weather. All have ample cooking utensils and dishes. Bed linens are furnished. Tea and bath towels are not furnished. Two full sized beds, with innerspring mattress, and one double sized roll-a-way bed are standard equipment, allowing comfortable occupancy for six persons. There are electric outlets to accommodate your radio and other appliances. There is also a coin operated radio for those who do not wish to bring their own. Five of our seven cottages are equipped with Frigidaire Air Conditioning Units. There is a play ground centrally located for smaller children. Every cottage is located on the lake-front, and a boat is included free of charge, with the rental of each cabin. Our cabins and water supply are approved by the State Board of Health.

● There are many natural cedar crappie beds and excellent coves for bass fishing close by. Many kinds of fish are caught in these waters; jack salmon, cat fish, blue gill, crappie, and white and black bass. The swimming is enjoyable here, as the water is clear of all moss and other rubbish. Also the swimming is safe for children, as the beach slopes gently into the water and there are no holes of sudden declines under the water. There are no mosquitoes to plague you while fishing or swimming or just enjoying the beautiful surroundings, as the Lake is sprayed periodically to eliminate these pests.

● An excellent restaurant is located within the camp grounds, where you may enjoy a pleasant meal or light snack on a spacious screened-in porch overlooking the resort and lake. Cold beer, ice cream, or light refreshments are served, and you are welcome to spend many pleasant hours with other vacationers, in cool, friendly surroundings. Groceries, cigarettes, candies, and fishing licenses may be secured here also. Live bait, motor gas and oil, and motors are also available.

● Catholic and Protestant churches are located within a short distance.

● SPECIAL - Spring & Fall Weekly Rates. $8.00 off on weekly reservations during May and September. $12.00 off on weekly reservations during Oct., Nov., March and April.

— RATES —

Cabins with one Sleeping Porch

	DAY	WEEK
2 Guests	$6.00	$38.50
4 Guests	$7.50	$48.50
6 Guests	$9.00	$58.50

Larger cabins with two sleeping porches.

	DAY	WEEK
4 Guests	$9.00	$54.50
6 Guests	$11.00	$65.50

$1.00 per day is added for each extra person. 50¢ for children under five years of age.

Motors are available for $4.00 per day or $20.00 per week.

LAKEWOOD SHORES

The Lake of the Ozarks

Star Route, Lake Rd. 16 — Versailles, Mo.

FOR RESERVATIONS WRITE—

LAKEWOOD SHORES
Star Route, Lake Rd. No. 16
Versailles, Mo.
PHONE — Sunrise Beach
Frontier 4-5360

TOM and SHIRLEY LONG, Proprietors

Check-out time is 2 o'clock, and check-in time 4 o'clock. You are invited to come earlier or stay later to enjoy the resort if you so desire. Please state exact time of arrival and departure, if possible.

No reservations are made for less than two days. A $10.00 deposit is requested to bind the reservation.

A 1950s-era lakeside resort advertising pamphlet. It is interesting to note the services, including Frigidaire Air Conditioning and a "coin operated" radio. Noteworthy also is the location south of Versailles, some twenty-two miles away. But the resort is actually in the Sunrise Beach area, just fifteen miles north of Camdenton and U.S 54. This ad description style is typical of the time, as Versailles was one of the largest towns in the area. *Author's private collection (KVL).*

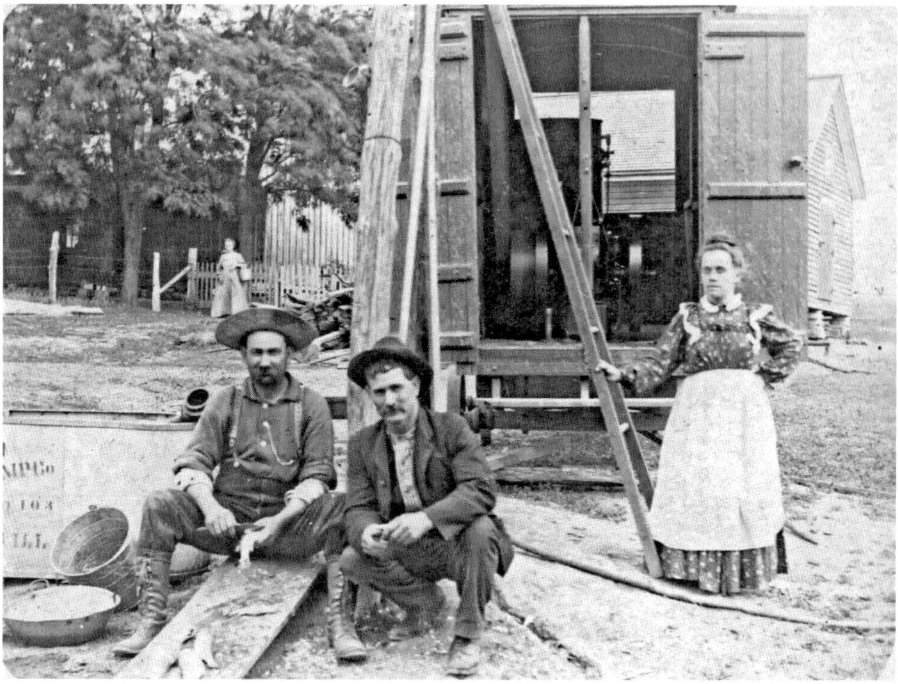

An early 1900s photo capture of work activity. One man is cleaning fish, and the two ladies are dressed in traditional garb, with one carrying a pail. They are all pictured near some type of power machine located along the Osage River. *Courtesy of Miller County Missouri Historical Society.*

region had in that instant changed forever. The tri-county area was overnight transformed from rural to urban in characteristics if not in character.

New boundaries appeared—what had been a short trek through mountainous terrain now became impassable except possibly by watercraft. The region immediately divided in commerce and community into "east side" and "west side" (of the lake—later these sides would become known as the "St. Louis side" and the "Kansas City side" respectively, signaling psychographic and political boundaries in addition to the physical divide imposed by the lake).

Where there had once been a limited menu of occupations—farmer, millworker, merchant (by the 1930s, the tie-hacking industry had faded away)—there would become available a panorama of possible positions. The first such positions were in construction on the dam and lake, and then within a few decades, careers in hospitality, medicine, real estate, retail sales and even such unimagined jobs as professional musician or instructor-performer in water sports would become accessible.

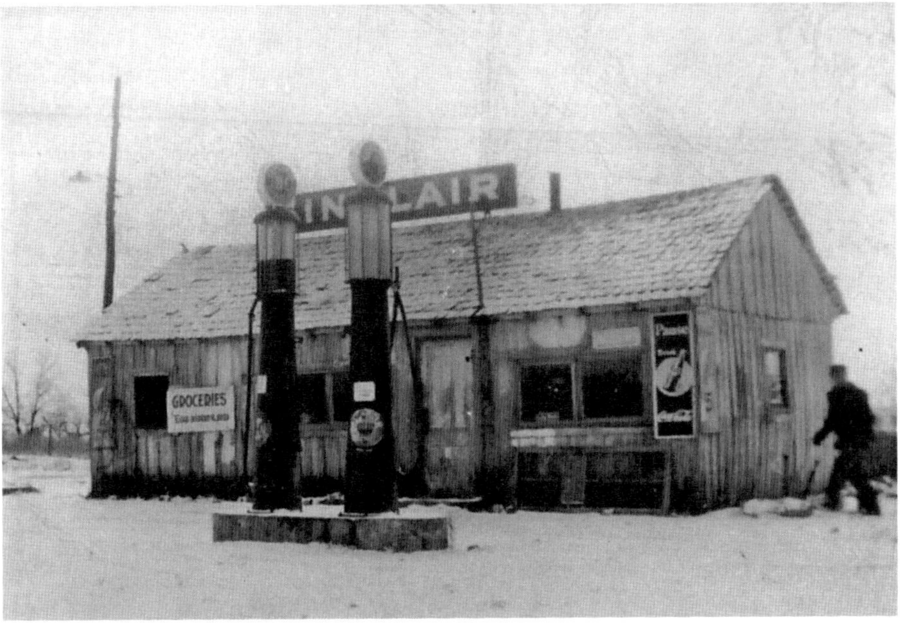

A basic rugged old store and station. A note with the photo indicates that many think this is the first business in Laurie, Missouri. Laurie is located south of Gravois Mills and north of Sunrise Beach on State Route 5. *Courtesy of Morgan County Historical Society.*

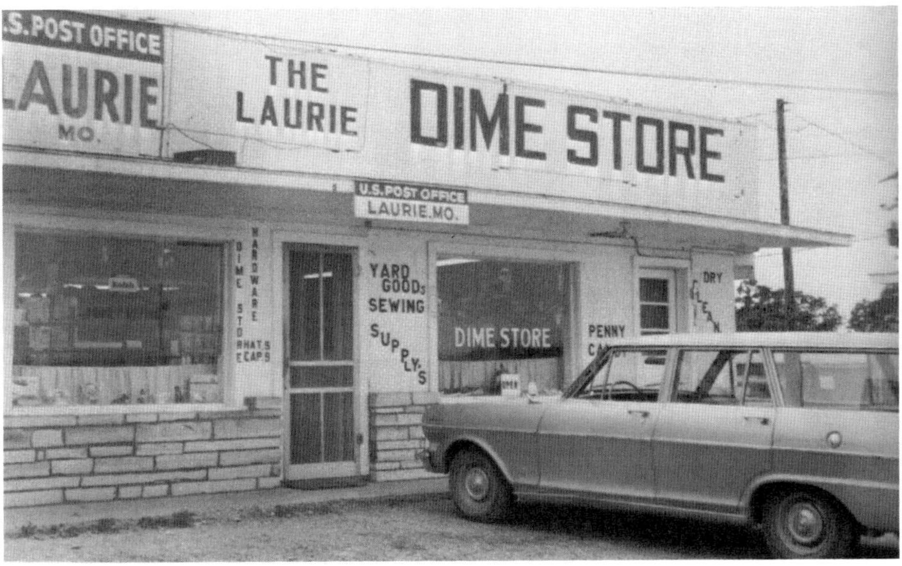

The U.S. Post Office was a side business for the Laurie Dime Store. This store carried caps, hats, hardware, sewing supplies and candy and provided dry cleaning service (most likely pick-up for a Versailles dry cleaner). It was very common to have the small-town post office placed in a local business establishment. *Courtesy of Morgan County Historical Society.*

Boundaries (psychological and physical) and diversity of occupational opportunities are two primary characteristics of urbanization and flow naturally from the urbanizing process (which is to say, proceed whether desired by the affected population or not). Other urban characteristics that do require conscious choice in reaction were present but would remain unaddressed or acted upon for decades. These included the necessity of cooperation in place of the mountain tradition of self-sufficiency, the need for government and regulation as well as an overarching regional infrastructure plan—in place of Ozarks laissez faire.

But in the early 1930s, concerns about the effects of urbanization in rural regions such as the Lake of the Ozarks were well on to a century distant. Those gazing into the mysterious green water of the lake at the time saw only their own reflections, perhaps framed in shimmering, mottled images of the sylvan hills and mountain skies above them.

Chapter 11

From Pistol Club to the Pen

Wealthy men from the city early on viewed the lake as a place to spend their extravagances and to conceal indiscretions.[1]

Ask any true local old-timer for his early recollections of the lake, and sooner than later he will mention the Ozark Pistol Club. Most will recall that it started in the early 1930s as the private club of a cluster of commodity traders from Kansas City. There was the grand log clubhouse with a huge open central room and an elegant fireplace; circular stairs led to a second-story balcony hall lined with sleeping rooms. There were a number of luxurious outlier cabins also.

At first awed, the locals were soon scandalized by open nudity and rumors of orgy. There was nothing to be done—it was said that powers like Kansas City political boss Tom Pendergast had helped finance the place, and Harry Truman had been a guest at one time. It was well beyond the control of local authorities.

The members customarily arrived in the impressive touring cars of the time, and when the Eighteenth Amendment was repealed the locals were said to have reported cases of liquor transported openly to the club.

There was a shooting range on the property, but the name "Pistol Club" was understood to be a cover for the real activities that went on. The club's alleged motto seems to bear that sense out: "Drink 'til Midnight, Pistol Dawn." It could be supposed that spouses and colleagues may have believed that it was just a shooting club—those were theoretically simpler times.

As years passed, the club became more open to the public, and the Williamses recall going to one of their high school dances there in the 1940s. The club—and the grand club building close by where the long lived but now gone Millstone Lodge (by the twenty-first century, it would become a condo complex retaining the Millstone name) would locate—finally vanished from the lake scene.

Meanwhile across the lake near Bagnell Dam, Union Electric executives were enjoying a similar clubhouse. Today known as Willmore Lodge, the structure was originally Egan's Lodge in honor of the president of UE, Louis H. Egan.

There is a persistent rumor—possibly due to his eventual criminal conviction on various counts, mostly having to do with a secret fund UE used to try to bribe politicians—that Egan was related to Tom and Willie Egan of the notorious "Egan's Rats" criminal organization that ruled the St. Louis underworld at the turn of the twentieth century. But no evidence of the connection is ever proffered.

Here it should be noted Egan, Street, Cravens and their associates and others discussed thus far were born in the latter decades of the nineteenth century.

Between the end of the Civil War and the New Deal—a period of over six decades and the era that informed the cultural attitudes of the early twentieth century—there was little or no government regulation or intervention in the activities of the commercial and industrial cultures in America. So business adventurers like Cravens and Egan may have had only vague concepts of criminality in the conduct of business.

Egan could even be presented as a victim of his times. Until the New Deal, no agency, governmental or otherwise, had paid much attention to his management of the various utility projects he was involved with. The secret slush fund he and other executives of UE and its corporate parent had set up to use for bribes to politicians and others had been conceived of in 1926—almost a decade before the federal regulations that braced the criminal complaint brought against him and UE. (Clearly, however, the UE executives knew from the beginning they were engaging in criminal behavior or they would not have operated the fund in secret.)

An important point is that if Egan could have magically transported to the early twenty-first century, the slush fund—openly distributed as political contributions—would have been perfectly legal. In 2010, the United States Supreme Court, in a 5–4 decision, ruled it quite permissible for corporate entities to make political contributions.[2]

But such magical transport being unavailable, in 1940, Egan and Union Electric were discovered in violation of a series of infractions. So it was that in 1943 the Eighth Circuit Court of Appeals—the same court appellant Walter P. Cravens had appeared before—heard Egan and UE together asking for a reversal of their separate convictions.

The appeals transcript recounts the case with clarity:

> *The plan to create a secret fund for use in making contributions to candidates for office and to political party committees by means of rebates and false expense accounts originated in 1926. In that year the subject was suggested to Boehm, executive vice president of Union Electric, by a Mr. Gruhl, then president of the parent holding company, the North American Company. The plan was developed and put in operation, and in 1932 the sum of $15,000 was contributed to the Republican national committee. The system continued in existence and operation until sometime in 1939 or 1940. During the period of its operation a fund of more than $591,000 was created by means of rebates and false expense accounts and expended through Boehm's office for political purposes in the interest of and for the benefit of Union Electric and its subsidiaries. It was distributed directly and indirectly to candidates for public office, to public officials, and to party committees in the states of Missouri, Illinois and Iowa by means of the mails, by the instrumentalities of interstate commerce and by delivery in person in the state of Missouri. The recipients included candidates for both federal and nonfederal offices, federal and nonfederal officials and both national and local party committees. Little if any party bias was shown in distributing these favors. Democrats and Republicans alike were among the beneficiaries.*

What is perhaps most interesting about UE and Egan's post-conviction appeal was the introduction of the moral issue of whether political contributions were "evil per se." The appellants said they were not. It had been Egan's contention throughout that all of his activity with the company had been innocent, and public relations related having nothing to do with the actual commerce of the company.

The court's dismissive response was that "it is axiomatic that innocent means may be used for an evil purpose."

Chapter 12
Egan's Aerie

That Louis H. Egan was in his time one of "the smartest guys in the room" cannot be diminished. He held an engineering degree from Yale University, and he ruled UE imperiously for years. His person radiated hauteur and physical dominance—the look of the alpha male. Doc Foster described Egan as a "big ole tall, red-haired fellow." Reporting Egan ruled foul of the law, in the July 29, 1940 issue of *Time* magazine, his height was recorded as "moose tall" and his demeanor as "aristocratic."

Under Egan's management, UE appears to have sought to gain monopoly on the electricity market in Illinois, Missouri and Iowa—hence the secret slush fund for political contributions.

Then having created a vast private recreational lake—after some debate in the Missouri legislature, the impoundment was christened the Lake of the Ozarks—Egan set about making it very, very comfortable for himself and his guests, of both the political and nonpolitical sort. Egan, through UE, bought a private airplane to shuttle executives and guests back and forth from various locales to the fabulous Adirondack-style lodge he had caused to be built on a promontory above the new dam.

A promotional booklet prepared by the Lake of the Ozarks Council of Local Government in 1981 describes the lodge:

> *That majestic log structure situated north of Bagnell Dam is known to people in the area as Willmore Lodge, although the Willmore Company was neither the first nor the last to own it.*

> *Built in 1930 as an administration building for the officials of the Union Electric Company, the lodge cost $135,000...although it took only three months to construct the preparation of the materials took two years.*
>
> *Hand hewn pine logs of the finest quality were brought in by rail from the state of Washington, and put together solely with wooden pegs.*

In other words, Egan wanted a custom-built, obviously extravagant, one-of-a-kind lodge—which he got.

Egan's Lodge was grand indeed. And to characterize it as an "administration building" requires considerable stretch. It was—like the Pistol Club a few miles across the lake—more of the nature of a party mansion than anything else.

For a few years in the 1940s, the property fell into disuse. Egan and most of his fellow executives were under indictment or jailed during that time, and the new governing powers of the company were apparently now sufficiently schooled in the ways of operating a regulated public utility that they seem to have avoided straying across criminal lines.

In the 1987 video, Al Elam stated that in 1945, one of the more stringent of the New Deal regulatory agencies, the Securities and Exchange Commission (SEC), forced the sale of the lake shoreline. This would have been, he noted, in accordance with the Public Utility Holding Company Act of 1935, which required that all public utilities engage only in the business of public utilities.

Thus the whole Lake of the Ozarks shoreline was put up for sale. That year, 1945, the utility abruptly sold the entire lakefront to a St. Louis real estate developer, Cyrus Crane Willmore.

The deal reportedly included (and reports vary somewhat) forty thousand acres of lakefront property and eight hundred miles of shoreline. To sweeten the deal, a hotel, a number of cottages and pleasure boats and Egan's majestic lodge—all owned by UE—were thrown in.

Final price for this vast purchase was an astoundingly low $320,000. It seems UE was just out to get shed of the property and out of the land development business.[1] And as it happens, Cyrus Willmore was indeed one of the most skilled real estate developers and promoters of his time.

Willmore rechristened the lodge "Willmore Lodge" and set about bringing developers and brokers from around the country for extravagant weekend barbeques and tours of the properties he wanted them to buy or develop.

The Willmore Company contracted with locals who had real estate expertise, notably Camden County's Al Elam and Morgan County's

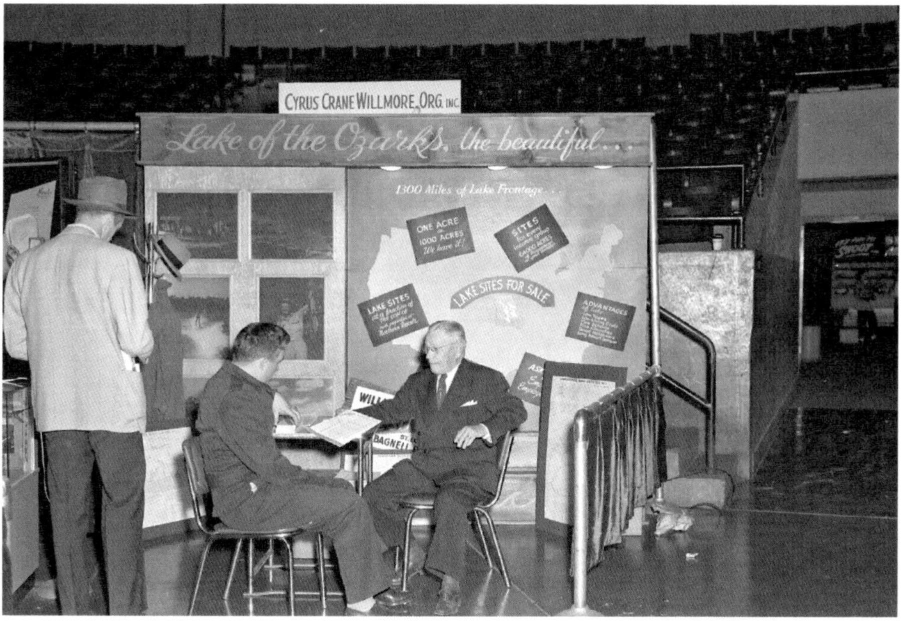

Cyrus Crane Willmore, Org. Inc. sales staff at a convention "pushing" lake lots for sale. *Courtesy of Missouri State Capitol Commission, Missouri State Archives.*

Russell P. Hall, to provide development and promotion. Elam was actually employed by the Willmore Company for a few years before forming his own organization: Al Elam Real Estate (the brand still carries enough weight decades later to appear prominently on the lake-area indicia of the company that now owns it).

Willmore also began constructing roads. He hired a youthful Lee Mace to work with Ernest McNeil, laying out, bulldozing and graveling roads in the properties adjacent to the dam area.

Willmore himself spent a great deal of time at the project, living in Willmore Lodge and driving over the roughed out roads and trails of the property in a pickup truck.

"Cy really wanted to be a country squire," Al Elam would later note. "He wanted to keep Horseshoe Bend and Shawnee Bend and sell the rest."

In 1998, Union Electric (Ameren UE) applied for designation of Willmore Lodge as a National Historic Place. The application document was prepared by Laura Johnson, preservationist, and Benjamin Cawthra, historian. The contribution of Willmore to the development of the lake was described thusly:

> *Willmore created the Lake of the Ozarks Lodge properties, and made plans for the development of the land. In the first couple of years after his purchase of the Union Electric property he created twenty-five miles of road on his property and began selling to other developers. In 1946, he initiated speed boat races on the lake to generate interest in the area's recreational possibilities.*

Passing note should be made of reports of earlier boat races at the lake—notably one in September 1935 at the Pistol Club designated grandly as the Lake of the Ozarks National Championship Boat Races. The total purse was $1,000—a goodly sum at the time. In the last quarter of the twentieth century, a high-profile race known as the Lake of the Ozarks Shootout had become a firmly established annual event, drawing competitors and spectators from around the globe.

Cy Willmore would die of a heart attack less than five years after what must have been the greatest deal of his career (indeed, one would think,

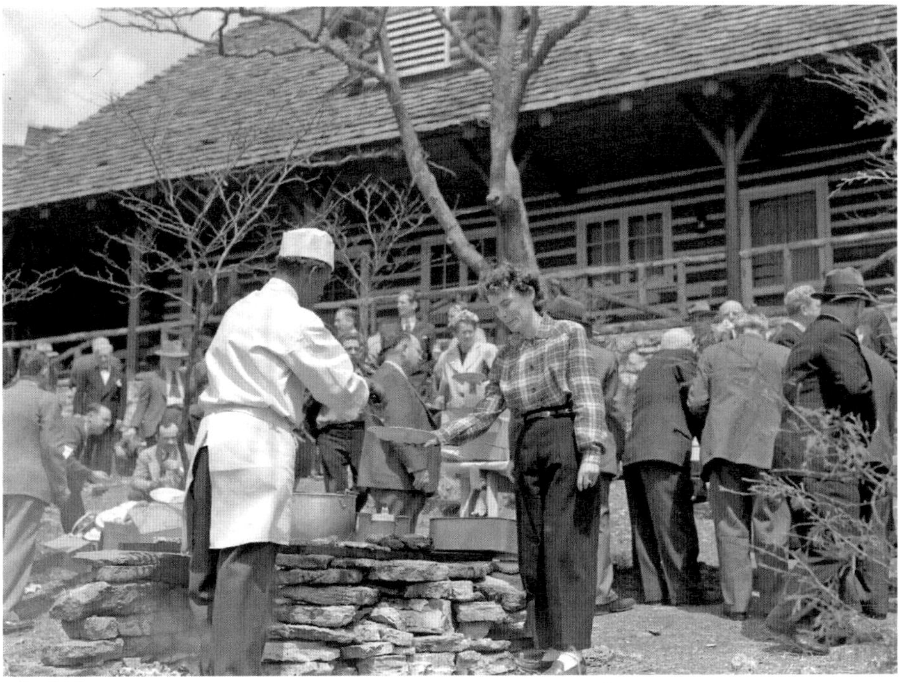

Willmore's private chef is shown preparing and serving a meal to a large convention group. This was a great day for Cyrus Willmore, as he enjoyed an opportunity to entertain a crowd. *Courtesy of Missouri State Capitol Commission, Missouri State Archives.*

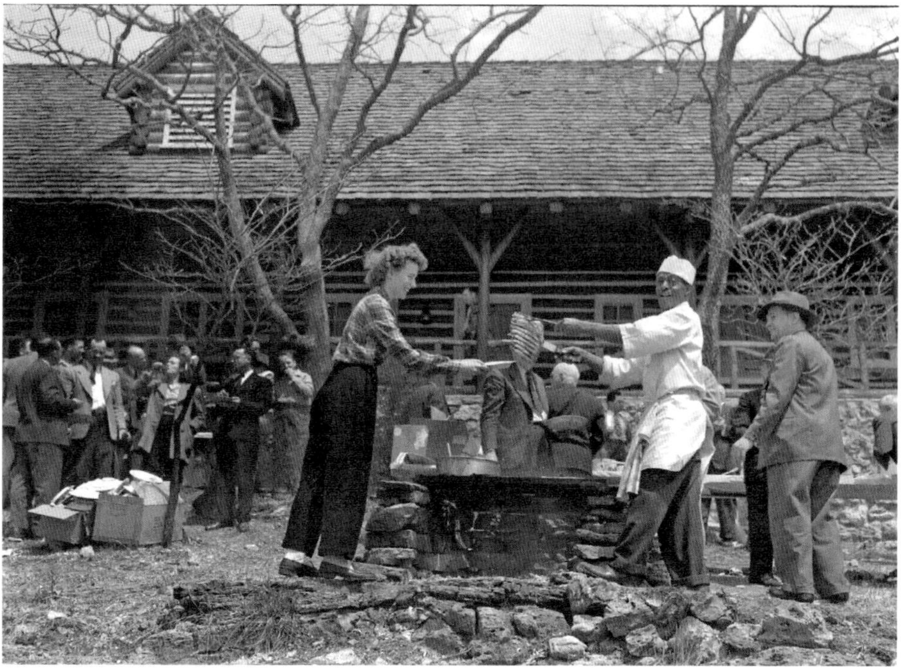

The chef is serving up ribs for the Willmores as they entertain. Cyrus Willmore had a strong desire to impress people. *Courtesy of Missouri State Capitol Commission, Missouri State Archives.*

of just about anyone's career). The Willmore Company would continue to operate, but it is said that his heirs did so unhappily and, like others so far presented, were probably glad when they finally parted with the burdensome lake properties.

Willmore Lodge was eventually repurchased by UE's successor company (Ameren) and put in service as a visitors' center and tourist attraction. It is listed in the National Register of Historic Places.

Willmore's obituary in the April 11, 1949 *St. Louis Globe Democrat* described him as "the last of the old time real estate promoters." This was, it seems, a truly accurate depiction.[2]

CHAPTER 13

THE STATUS OF FORCES

For much of American history, veterans of wars have been more or less forgotten as soon as peace was settled. This tradition extends from the founding of the First Republic when George Washington was forced to persuade mutinying Continental army officers—concerned with being denied promised benefits—from rebellion with his declaration that he had "not only grown gray but almost blind in the service of my country."

George Patton, an army major in the 1930s, rode horseback, Cossack-style, into masses of protesting World War I veterans in Washington, D.C., seeking early payment on promised bonuses to help them ease the hardships of the Great Depression (the "Bonus Army"). Patton is said to have relished the experience, leaning forward in his saddle to sharply spank whatever old soldiers he could reach with the flat of his sword.

There have been numerous reports of soldiers returning from the Vietnam Conflict being treated with abuse and neglect at the hands of fellow citizens and various government agencies.[1]

The singular exception in the history of America post-bellum attitude toward the nation's warriors is that of World War II. In 1944, Franklin Roosevelt signed the GI Bill into law ("Servicemen's Readjustment Act"). The principal effect of this legislation was to create a super privileged segment of the population—elevated or secured at solid middle-class status—and doing so for a goodly number who would have had little or no chance of achieving such station without this unprecedented government propeller.[2]

Although unprecedented in execution, the GI Bill was in fact a version of a public benefit program that Franklin Delano Roosevelt had long envisioned. The difference between the bill and FDR's never realized New Deal dream was that Roosevelt would have extended many of the benefits of the bill to a much broader segment of American society.

Only those who served in uniform in the war were extended GI Bill benefits—which indeed did not even then take note of all who suited up or faced peril in their country's service. The Women Airforce Service Pilots (WASPs) were finally extended GI benefits in the late 1970s—the Merchant Marine never.[3] The sacrifices made by the civilian population—"Rosie the Riveter" and others—were simply taken for granted by the bill or (in an alternate view) ignored.

About half of the sixteen million eligible World War II veterans took advantage of the education benefits—essentially any kind of education: university, vocational or otherwise.[4]

In addition to liberal support in obtaining advanced education, the government benefits extended to veterans of World War II provided substantial subsidies for everything from lifelong healthcare to low-rate home mortgages.

Being relieved of the necessity of accumulating funds for expenses like down payments or tuition costs and being the recipients of lifelong medical care meant the GI Bill beneficiaries and the generally financially buoyed balance of the American population—postwar prosperity owed much to the fact that a great deal of the rest of the world's production infrastructure had been destroyed—could turn to investment, to business endeavors and to recreational pursuits that might have been improbable without the government subsidies of the bill to private citizens and would have been unheard of in the Depression era.

Recreation- and leisure-related activities and products in America—specifically middle-class oriented—were about to become big business. It is no coincidence the Weber Grill made its debut in the early 1950s. At about the same time, the "house trailer" of the 1930s and '40s was reinvented as what would soon become the "recreational vehicle" ("RV").

Milton Rafferty described the change in the leisure culture in America: "After World War II the Sunday-afternoon spin, which had become popular before the war was replaced by the weekend trip; the vacation tour could easily span the continent."

It was in this time of change that the first visible signs of urbanization began to manifest around the lake. Occupations that were alien to the "old" lake culture appeared. For example, it is unlikely any of the locals had performed tricks on water skis before Willmore's exhibitions of the sport began, and the appearance of RVs must have caused some curiosity with the locals. But most importantly, diverse occupations not available in the past began to present—real estate sales, hospitality industry work, construction jobs related to both residential and commercial development. This diversity would be the harbinger of the then invisible but nonetheless inevitable urban overlay that would come to characterize lake society.

As previously noted, the war's end and postwar social change had found Cyrus Crane Willmore positioned to profit from the postwar leisure boom—and he clearly knew it. Prior to Wilmore's death, the Willmore Company had aggressively built lake access roads, sponsored water ski exhibitions and promoted the newly acquired fiefdom (the shoreline of—and unfettered access to—the Lake of the Ozarks) to the newly prospering American consumer class, wherever they might be. For the first time, the Lake of the Ozarks was marketed aggressively to the cities of the Midwest. Kansas City,

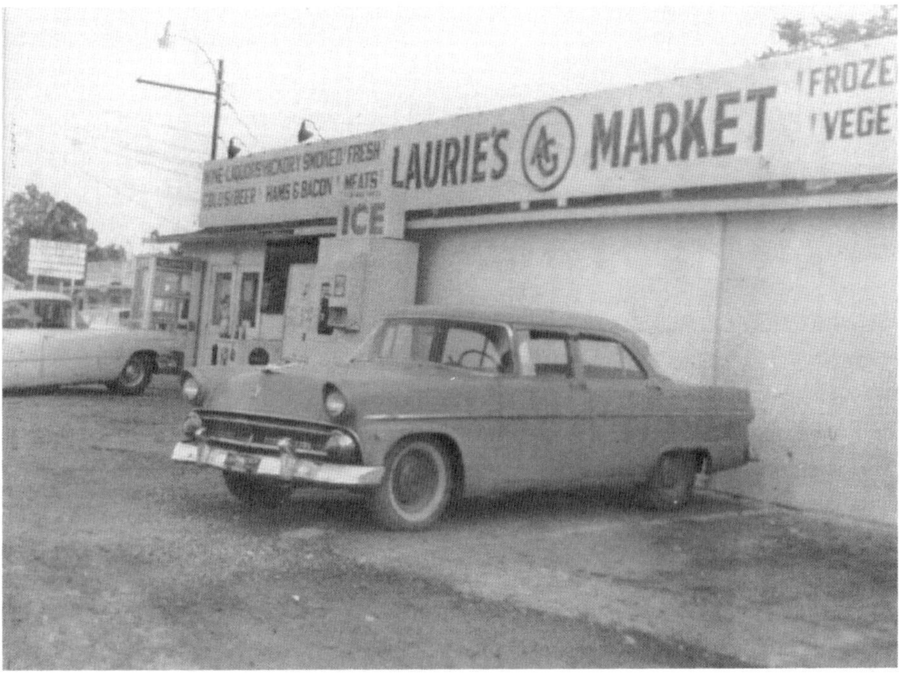

This 1950s photo depicts storefront signs that show everything available at the market, including food, beer, sprits and groceries. Although the signs don't show it, most of these local stores also had hunting and fishing licenses for sale. *Courtesy of Morgan County Historical Society.*

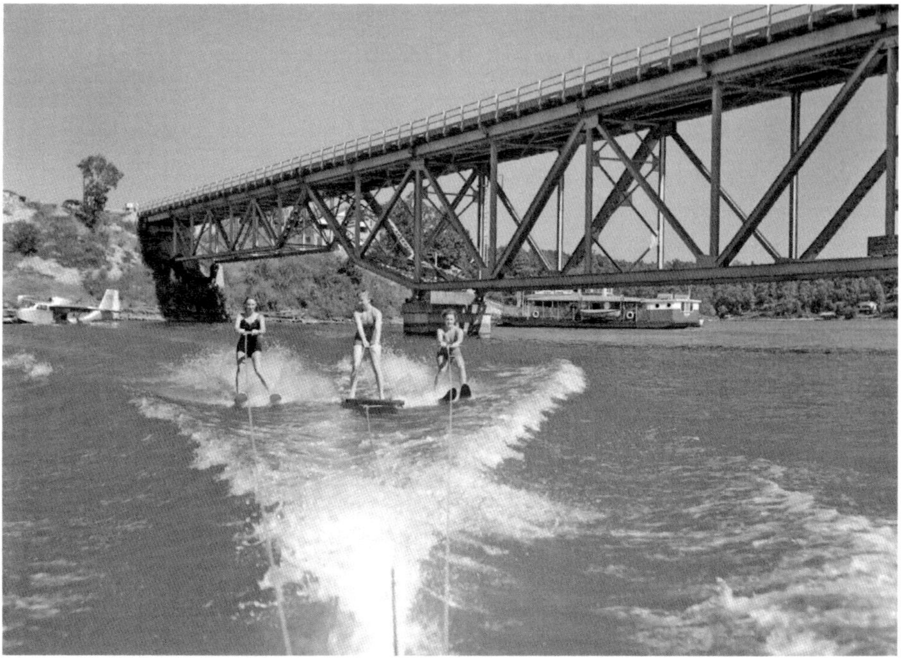

A group enjoying water-skiing on the lake. In the background is the recognizable upside-down Hurricane Deck bridge and an excursion boat. *Courtesy of Missouri State Capitol Commission, Missouri State Archives.*

St. Louis and Chicago were made aware of the recreational playground that lay within driving distance of their doors.[5]

Cy Willmore, briefly the prince of the lake and ensconced in his rustic palace on the palisades overlooking Bagnell Dam, had by that time begun conferring baronies on a chosen cadre who had the know-how to develop his principality—to make the until then mostly idle lakefront property a sought-after asset among the emerging postwar middle class.

Foremost of Wilmore's associates were two men who could be considered among the principal founders of the lake's fortunes: Russell P. Hall of Morgan County and Albert Gray Elam of Camden County.

Russell Hall's son, Robert (Bob), a retired medical doctor, recalled his father's role in the development of the lake in a personal reminiscence written in 2013:

> *Russell P. Hall...had graduated from the University of Illinois, Urbana in 1914, and while a student there, he became acquainted with fellow student,*

Cyrus Crane Willmore. This chance relationship, though casual, proved to be important in the 1940s.

Russell moved his family to Versailles in 1931, after taking a job with a Quincy, Illinois bank to dispose of the 100 plus farms that the bank had foreclosed on during those early Depression years. He worked to try to keep the foreclosed farmers on their farms and earned considerable local respect for this effort.

As the Lake area started to come back to life as a resort and retirement area, Russell came into contact with Al Elam of Lake Ozark, who was beginning to work as the Willmore Lake Properties sales development agent. Russell immediately connected with the Willmore Company and was soon the agent for the Gravois arm and west lake area of the burgeoning Willmore Company.

Russell began to develop subdivisions in the Gravois and Sunrise Beach areas, first buying tracts of shoreline property and then doing the actual developing. Willmore Properties sold these tracts on liberal terms

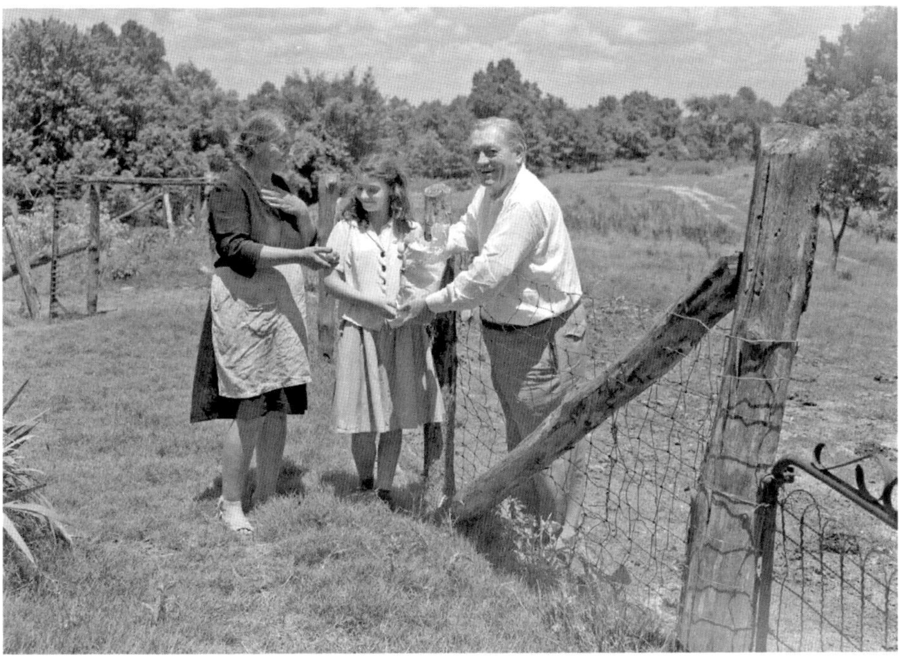

There are stories of Cyrus Willmore wanting to be a farmer and purchasing several acres of local land. In this photo, Cyrus is talking with two ladies and is getting a bag of fresh peaches. He is probably trying to be neighborly. They must all be pleased, judging by the smiles on their faces. *Courtesy of Missouri State Capitol Commission, Missouri State Archives.*

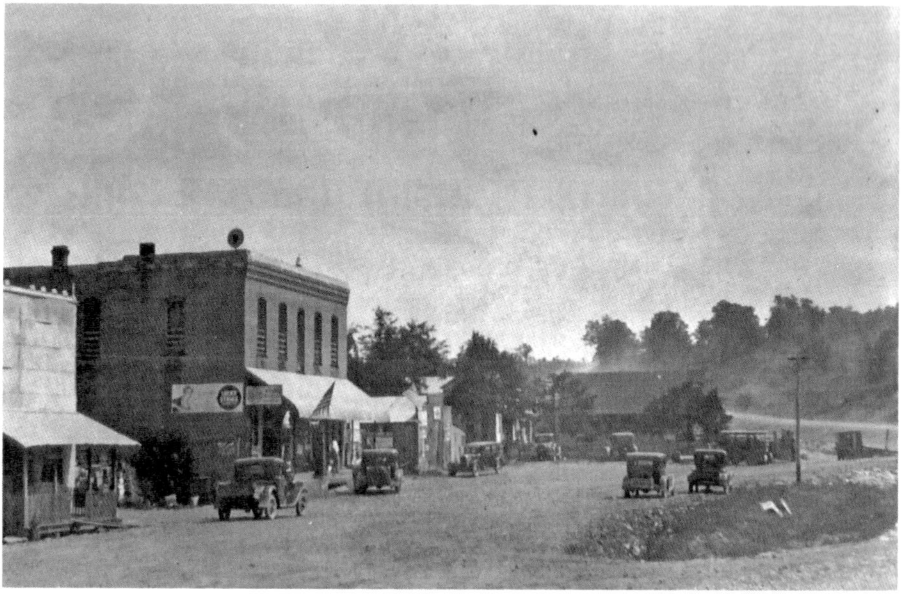

Gravois Mills is one of the oldest communities in the lake area. Gravois Mills, served by the Troutdale (Collins) Spring and the Big and Little Gravois Creeks, provided mill water power and services long before the lake was built. *Courtesy of Morgan County Historical Society.*

> *to Russell since the company wanted to dispose of the many hundreds of tracts as a business decision. After Mr. Willmore died unexpectedly, the sales group headed by Al Elam continued the wide spread* [sic] *developments...until the eventual sale of much of Horseshoe and Shawnee Bends to the Koplar interests.*
>
> *I knew Al Elam quite well and he was the consummate salesman. His wife was called "Skeeter" as I recall. The sales group of Willmore Properties had a New Year's Eve party in Lake Ozark for several years and my parents enjoyed that group as long as that continued.*
>
> *One of the big bends of the Osage River was known as Coffman Bend. It was further upstream and was later to sell. Harold Gunn of Sedalia, Nolan Helm of Camdenton and my father partnered to buy and develop the huge property.*

Gunn and Helm financed the project, and Hall was the developer who constructed the roads, arranged for platting and sold the lots.

> *This project took years to complete but was highly profitable for all three parties. This project was done with a handshake and to my memory there*

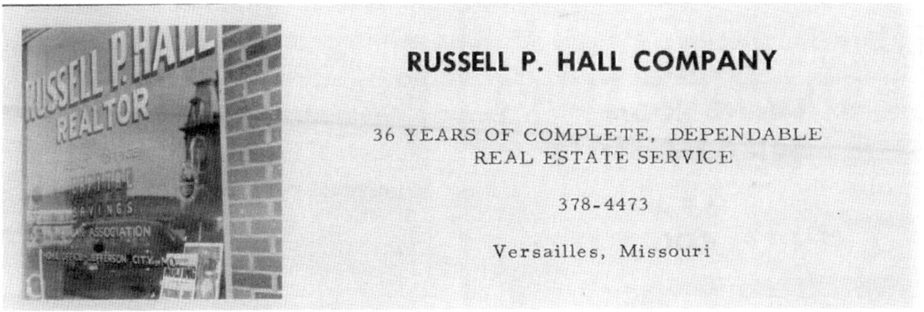

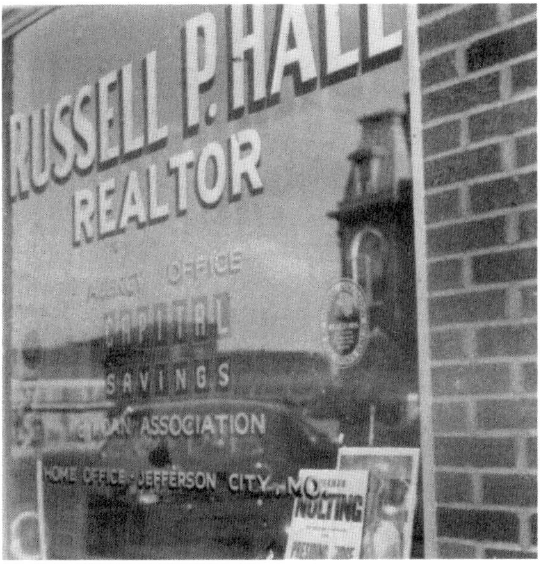

Russell P. Hall was a major player in property development on the lake's north and west sides. *Courtesy of Morgan County Historical Society.*

was never a disagreement of importance. Ralph Vincent of Camdenton did survey work here and for many other properties for Russell. Dexter Slagle did this work for us later, especially in Morgan County.

During the early years Mr. Willmore loved to entertain his St. Louis contacts with parties at the Lake to promote his vision of its development. During the summer of 1946 or '47 I remember attending a big barbecue he arranged on the shores of the then absolutely undeveloped Shawnee Bend. There was an old gravel road into Shawnee Bend and some level shoreline suitable for boat beaching for the folks who would arrive from Willmore Lodge by boat. My father was in charge of the barbecue event and actually was the head chef. Russell loved to do things like this and I was proud to be there with him. I was about twelve and my brother Jim, age eleven, was also there…I remember Mr. Willmore as a very gregarious host with an imposing voice and a full head of sandy red hair.

Russell P. Hall served as president of both the Lake of the Ozarks Association and the Lake of the Ozarks Board of Realtors. In private correspondence with the authors, Bob Hall estimated his father developed at least twenty-five residential lakeshore subdivisions while also selling existing lake homes to "huge numbers of folks from Iowa, Kansas, Illinois, and all over Missouri."

Chapter 14

Those Kids and the (Not) Hillbillies

The first effect of the urbanization of the Lake of the Ozarks region came at once with the commencement of construction at the dam site. The diversification of occupational availability was immediate, and with it came a flow of outsiders with the required skill sets—and the outsiders often relocated their families to the lake.[1] One true local who witnessed those times—speaking in the early twenty-first century—provided insight based on her experience as a schoolchild in the 1930s.

(KVL) The Bagnell Dam Project included the building of facilities to serve the workers. This site, on the hilltop bluff, east side of the dam, was called the "construction camp." The site included a commissary, hospital and living facilities—that is, dormitories and cabins. These facilities housed construction workers and their families.

As the dam construction wound down, some workers and their families continued living at the facilities as employees of Union Electric. They remained for many years, serving as UE employees.

One of the impacts this population exerted on the area was the founding of a "consolidated" public school district. Several of the one-room schools were shuttered and a central school building constructed: the School of the Osage. (The original structure, although modified, still serves the district.) This facility was located on the west-side hill at the dam, an area that became known as "the strip."

This west side of the dam area grew with the building of structures serving local working and visiting populations. The area included stores, eating establishments, a water tower and a theater. Many of these residents were local families relocated out of the bottoms when the water began to rise. They had to find new sources of income, changing from an agrarian lifestyle to other means of making a living. The permanence of construction workers and Union Electric families brought recognition by the local residents of "outside people" who were strangers to the local culture.

My conversation with a true local born and reared on the west-side hill at the dam provided insight to the recognized difference between the locals and non-locals. She identified original business owners and residents along what is now "the strip." She added, "I went to school at Osage, all through grade school and high school. Us kids who were born and reared in the area, called the kids from the construction camps east of the dam 'those kids.' We felt they were not part of our local heritage."

This is an important recognition by the local multigenerational families—as early as the late 1930s and into the 1940s—of the difference between long-term local family heritage and those new residents to the area.

It is evident there was recognition that the lake area was destined for permanent change—a change that supported area economic development and led to urban characteristics as early as the late 1930s and early '40s, long before anyone envisioned the dynamic development of the lake area over the next fifty years.

Probably due to the influence of the urbanizing lake region, the Osage school described earlier was consolidated and modernized long before Missouri's school district reorganization of the 1950s and 1960s.

No doubt "those kids" regarded the locals with the same sense of schism as that voiced by the above quoted informant—very possibly considering the surrounding culture as the realm of the "hillbilly." At the risk of stating the obvious, not everyone who lives in the Ozarks is a hillbilly. There is a distinct and definable character to the genus, but "real" hillbillies in the Ozarks are a minority.

Writing in the late 1940s, Vance Randolph expressed a view of Ozark society that is most useful to this narrative: "The people who live in the Ozark country of Missouri and Arkansas were until recently, the most deliberately unprogressive people in the United States." Folklorist Randolph assigned too narrow a region and time frame to the description of this "unprogressive" cultural character—it is, in fact, a statewide attitude in Missouri.

Brooks Blevins, a professor at Missouri State University in Springfield, has written extensively about Ozarks life and customs. In his book *Arkansas/Arkansaw,* he enumerated the specific qualities of the hillbilly, noting foremost that all hillbillies are white people—an obvious but sometimes overlooked fact.

Modern-day Ozarks hillbillies continued to live in the margins of society and are still more or less invisible as real people to the general culture. Their lifestyle remained pretty much that of the lilies of the field—still in a clannish hunter-gatherer tradition and generally leading precarious fiscal existences. Wild greens, deer and wild turkey, as well as small game and pan fish, played a role in many backwoods diets, but by the latter decades of the century, most hillbillies procured their bread, frozen dinners and such at supermarkets or food banks just like everyone else.

Into the next century, Ozark housing still frequently included the ofttimes off-kilter, plywood or pressed-board constructions associated with the region's older tar paper "shack" or "shed" housing architecture, but the build out was most often anchored to a manufactured or mobile structure (commonly referred to as a single- or double-wide; in earlier days, these structures were referred to as "shell homes").

The fact is by the late twentieth and early twenty-first centuries, the majority of Ozarkers bore but slight resemblance to stereotypical hillbillies but were, rather, hardworking farmers, construction and factory workers, tradespeople, accountants and so forth—in other words, just like the American mainstream but in a rural setting.

Because there is less opportunity for wages in rural sectors of the country, the labor that was offered there was often hard and less lucrative than urban occupations.[2]

Traditionally, the division of labor in rural life was defined mostly based on gender. The female had the responsibilities of the upkeep of the house and domestic grounds and the training of female children in these and other necessary duties—gardening, gathering and canning, as example. The male was responsible for hunting and raising crops; caring for the land, livestock and buildings; and the training of the male children in this "man's work."

Prior to the 1950s, many rural Ozark children received formal education only up to the sixth- or eighth-grade level in one-room country schools. This did not necessarily signify that education was not valued, but for rural families prior to the 1950s, sending a child to high school meant somehow paying for room and board in town during the school months.

Many rural young men entered the military for a tour—with an urgency that found them often concealing the fact they were underage for such service—as an escape from restlessness and boredom as well as a passage to adulthood before returning to the farm.

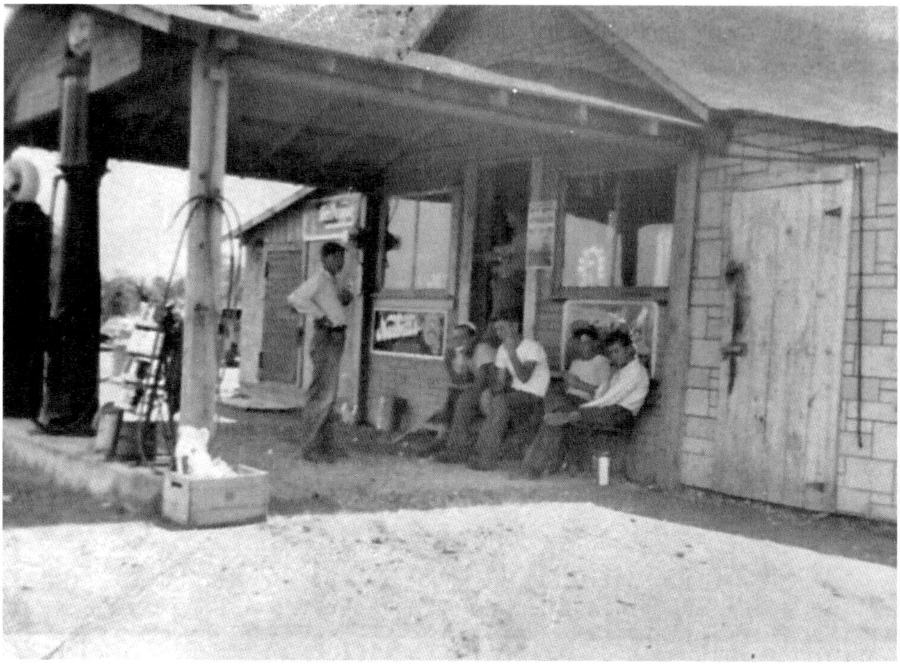

This Morgan County gas station was the "local gathern'" place. *Courtesy of Morgan County Historical Society.*

Young women were expected to marry as soon as possible. A marriage "hope chest"—containing household items, most often linens and flatware—was stored for them at a young age. A common phrase when discussing a prospective husband or wife was what they would "bring to the marriage"—in the rough hands of rural life, emotional issues such as love or desire were sometimes viewed at a considerable discount by comparison to the gain of scarce possessions or property through marital alliances.

As a cultural rule, adult life was generally expected to follow the pattern of previous generations. By mid-twentieth century, however, the traditional life pattern broke most notably in that one or both of the household heads was often seeking employment outside the farm, and modern "reorganized" school districts were busing rural children to central schools for "compulsory" education.

Changes in basic needs, wants and demands required both men and women to be able to perform several different types of chores to keep the rural (farm) homeplace going. There were increasingly fewer gender-specific activities or, for that matter, work related to the farm-based household. This change was manifest in several sometimes subtle ways; making and baking of bread as a matter of domestic course, for example, became increasingly rare. Cash-money wages, though, enabled the household to purchase store-bought bread—in the Ozarks, the designation of which was "light bread." Both terms were soon seldom heard as routine home baking became more the exception than the rule.

Sometimes the seeking of cash employment required the seeker move to or closer to an urban center. Further cultural interference arose from the fact that the available wage work frequently required skills unrelated to rural life. Traditional farm education was of little use in these instances.

Chapter 15

LEE MACE

One of the most important figures in the history of the Lake of the Ozarks, Lee Mace, a native of Miller County, Missouri, was born in 1927. His father, Lucian, was a prominent citizen, twice elected to the state legislature and who also did a stint as Miller County sheriff.[1]

Lee Mace exhibited musical talent early on, learning to play traditional Ozark music on guitar and fiddle as a child. His sister, Lois Mace Webb, described youthful Lee's introduction to music making in the 1930s and early 1940s.

"We were off in some corner, inconspicuous as possible," Webb recalled, noting that the process was to listen to learn the rhythm and changes of the fiddle tunes and then slowly take a place with the musicians—if so desired, though Webb noted she was never tempted to make music. But Lee soon moved into the chair beside the fiddlers."

(Note the similarity to the "follerin'" aspect of farm skills learned in those times described by Wise.)

Webb went on to say, "Lee asked Mother to show him some guitar chords…He learned easily, he understood the 'changes' and it wasn't long until he too could 'second' for the fiddlers."

Webb then explained how it was that her family danced—a form of entertainment proscribed by much of the Ozarks old-time religions: "Our family was one of several known as 'dancing Baptists.' Anyone who wanted to go to the trouble would have a dance on Saturday night. One or two rooms were cleared completely of furniture. There was always someone in the neighborhood who could 'play for a dance.' Many people could play…but not everyone could 'play for a dance'…his was a talent that was not lightly overlooked."

By the late 1940s, Lee and a group of his friends—including his future wife, Joyce Williams—created an art of the traditional dance of the Ozarks, a Celtic-style jig, including putting taps on their dancing shoes to make the steps even livelier. The troupe was soon barnstorming the picnic (county fair) circuit throughout the Missouri and Arkansas Ozarks. The mesmerizing dance the group performed was known as the "Ozark Jig," though Lee Mace called it the "Ozark Mountain Jig."

It wasn't long before the young dancers found the national stage. By the early 1950s, the jig dance troupe, known as the Lake of the Ozarks Square Dancers, had appeared on national television shows—twice on *Ted Mack's Amateur Hour* and the *Today Show* with Dave Garroway—and had headlined at the Blue Room in New Orleans for a month and at the Riverside in Reno, Nevada.

Additionally, they had played nationally noted venues like the Chicago Fair and the Kansas City Centennial. But most significantly, the troupe had been hired by the Grand Ole Opry to perform as "The Grand Ole Opry Square Dancers."

The poster proclaiming the troupe's performance in Reno explains a great deal of their appeal: "Real Old Fashioned 'Hoe Downs' to the Tune of the Six Piece Hill-Billy Symphony! SOMETHING ENTIRELY NEW IN ENTERTAINMENT!"

Of course, Ozark jig dancing was entirely new only to those unfamiliar with Ozarks culture—which is to say most of the country.

By the time Lee and Joyce had reached their mid-twenties, they were well established in Nashville. They appeared as regulars on over one hundred *Grand Ole Opry* episodes (still available in Technicolor video under various titles, including "The Albert Gannaway Collection") and had solid contacts in the emerging country music industry.

But the pair left Nashville and returned to Miller County, settling in Osage Beach, a few miles from where Lee had grown up. There Lee worked as program director and DJ at KRMS-AM, a recently founded radio station, while he and Joyce and the Jig Dance troupe commuted to Nashville to complete the Gannaway contract.

In those days—the early 1950s—live music was still very much a part of radio airplay. Lee quickly established a regularly scheduled show that he dubbed *The Ozark Opry*, featuring himself on acoustic bass with a band of bluegrass musicians.

The popularity of the radio show convinced Lee and the station's management in 1953 to commence regularly scheduled live shows in the Lakeside Casino building at the west end of Bagnell Dam. The shows were instantly successful, and Lee purchased the rights to the show's title from the radio station.

In 1957, the Maces constructed a one-thousand-seat auditorium on Highway 54, a few miles from the dam. Thus came about a fifty-three-year run of Ozark Opry shows that in season ran six to eight times a week, as well as a weekly television show that ran for thirty years and a vigorous off-season touring schedule.

One of the most significant features of the Maces' venture was that "Lee Mace's Ozark Opry" was the first show to feature the same ensemble cast of musicians—with no "star" performers—playing the same repertoire at each show, with six to ten shows a week in season. This concept would hold audiences for decades and, significantly, would provide the template for what would be termed "Branson-style" entertainment, for the town in

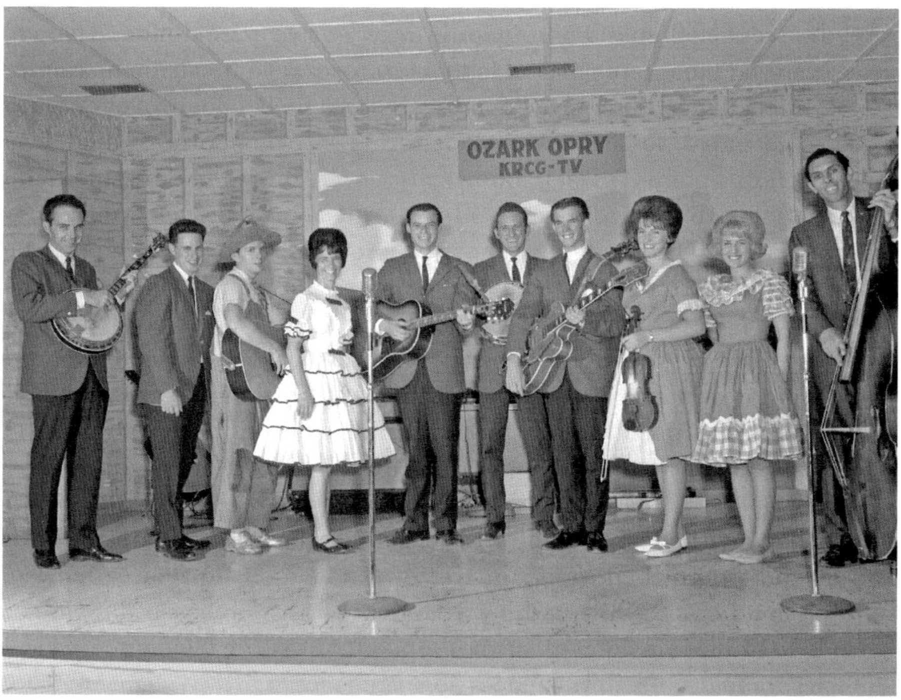

Lee Mace was an early visionary for the lake with his music show, including a weekly broadcast on local television. Mace was instrumental in area development enterprises. *Courtesy of Missouri State Capitol Commission, Missouri State Archives.*

southwestern Missouri where the format provided the basis for musical entertainment venues established between 1959 and the 1970s. Between 1959 and 1980, there were five such venues in Branson.

But the narrative should reset here to an unaddressed issue: if Lee and Joyce Mace were successes in Nashville, what was the motive for returning to the Ozarks?

By the late 1950s, the word "hillbilly" had been banished from Nashville, replaced by the more market-friendly "Country and Western" designation. With notable contrarianism, Mace promoted the Ozark Opry by driving his Buick through the tourist areas around Bagnell Dam with a blaring loudspeaker on top inviting the world to come see his "hillbilly" show.

He composed a theme song for the show:

Howdy all you friends and neighbors
Welcome to our hillbilly show
Tune up the five-string banjo
Take down the fiddle and the bow
Roll back the rug in the parlor
Light up the corncob pipe
Everyone is going to have some fun
At the Ozark Opry tonight

Lee would note several times over the years, "When folks came to the lake, the first thing they wanted to see was the Dam and the next was a hillbilly. We thought we'd show them a hillbilly even if we had to go to Chicago and hire one."

But the "hillbilly" show was not just clever marketing—although it was, in fact, marketing genius since the city folk tourists of the 1950s and 1960s would have had little interest in a "country" music show but indeed flocked to see a "hillbilly" show. Lee's attitude toward his music indicates a deeper connection to the Ozark culture than might have been noted. He wasn't just a guy who put together a musical entertainment troupe whose members dressed as rustics and told country jokes for the patronage of tourists from the city. Lee had a distinct musical agenda that was firmly rooted in the values of the Ozarks.

Toward the end of his life, Lee brought his niece Vickie Sparkman into the Ozark Opry cast. In discussion of how he required his performers to approach the music, he told her, "We shouldn't change the old songs, because they would be something else from what they were meant to be if we did."

Compare this statement to the following quote from the text of the popular folklore course presented by the eminent ethnographers Keith and Kathryn Cunningham at Northern Arizona University:

> *Neil Morris was interviewed by John Quincy Wolf, the folklorist from Lyon College in Arkansas in the 1950s. Dr. Wolf asked if Mr. Morris ever edited his traditional songs, and Mr. Morris said "No, a singer doesn't deliberately change his songs. He may forget a word here and there and put in other words, but if he remembers a song the way his parents sang it, he will not change it." Later on Mr. Morris added, "As for me, I change my songs as little as anybody."*[2]

Knowing that Lee Mace shared and was determined to preserve traditional Ozark values is critical to an understanding of the probable reasons he did not remain in the Nashville fold back in the 1950s and what his plans might have been for a next generation of "Country" music.

Chapter 16

THE MARVEL MODEL

Early in the twenty-first century, a project was undertaken to create a modern multi-lane freeway system through the Osage Beach area, by then an urban amalgam of resorts, residential housing and retail businesses adjacent to the town of Lake Ozark, the Osage River and Bagnell Dam.

On a bluff overlooking the entrance to the maze of bypasses and pavement blasted into and along the wooded escarpments that had formerly characterized a drive through the town, a bright white lettered sculpture appeared, modeled on the iconic "Hollywood" sign made famous in the hills of the California cinema city. LAKE OF THE OZARKS is prominently proclaimed.

The new freeway enabled complete circumvention of the entirety of Osage Beach by automobile and thus shaved as much as thirty-minutes from through travel. This, with other highway improvements to the south, reduced the drive time to Branson, Missouri, from the Lake of the Ozarks to about two hours, down from three or more.

In the course of the twentieth century, the Missouri Ozarks had experienced a somewhat curious phenomenon: two urban regions had sprouted in the wild, both with no planning or provision for urban stresses and demands. Neither had originally given any thought to orderly implementation of the kind of municipal services characteristic of more considered urban areas.

Although both regions shared the Ozark culture and traditions, the approach each took to exploiting its unique resources was of distinctly different focus. The Lake of the Ozarks initially sought to attract a

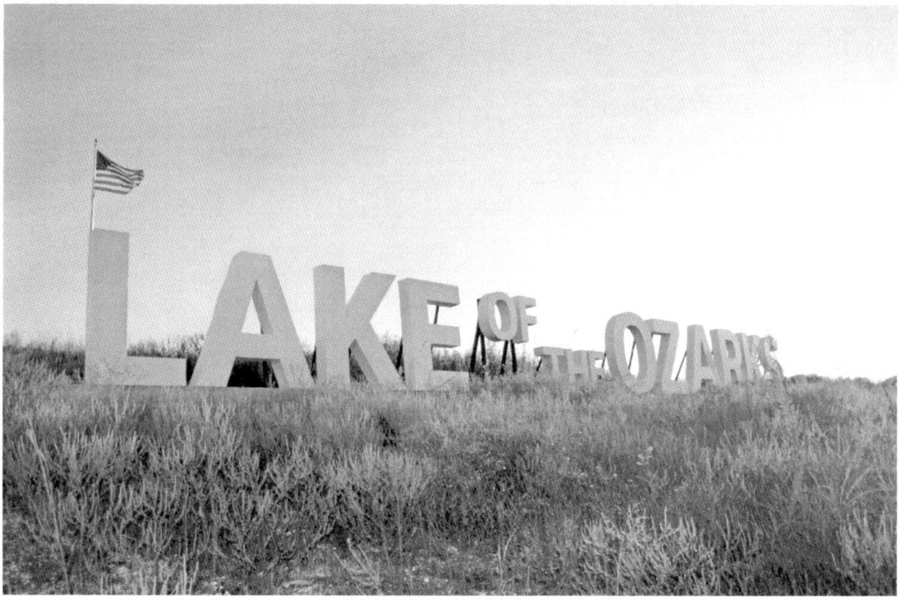

Patterned after the famous Hollywood sign, this lighted sign accents the entire Lake of the Ozarks area. Located along U.S. 54 at the Osage River below the Bagnell Dam, the sign is lighted and also changes colors. *Courtesy of Lake Area Chamber of Commerce.*

permanent, part-time, vacation home–dwelling, recreation-seeking population (that is, seeking participatory pastime offerings like fishing, boating and so on), while the Shepherd of the Hills region—after a time more readily identified as "Branson"—sought tourism-based commerce in the form of non-permanent but repeat (and referral) resort- or motel-dwelling visitors seeking passive, guided entertainment—most notably music-centered shows as the region matured.

When viewed from a sociological or cultural history perspective, the commercial direction each of these regions chose seems inevitable.

The southwestern stretch of the Ozarks—Taney, Stone and Christian Counties, the region of the White River—had been a tourist and spa destination for a half century before the construction of Bagnell Dam and its resultant recreational lake. The Branson–White River area is the part of the region we refer to herein as the "exterior Ozarks."

Though mountainous, the White River region—in addition to having more accommodating waterways for steamboats—was sufficiently plateaued with contiguous glade, ledge and valley stretches to enable development of transportation means that the more rugged interior Ozarks deterred or denied.[1]

By the late nineteenth century, tourists were floating and hiking throughout the White River region, with Marvel Cave (originally "Marble Cave") serving as a principal destination. A lengthy stay in the area was also frequently prescribed by physicians in Midwestern cities as a cure for various physical ailments.

So it was that early in the twentieth century, Harold Bell Wright arrived in the Branson area for the purpose of taking such a cure and, while doing so, found the inspiration for his novel *The Shepherd of the Hills,* published in 1907.[2] Wright let it be known that the hillbilly characters and rustic settings in the story were largely modeled on real characters and places he had encountered during his Ozarks sojourn.

In short, tourists could not only visit the exotic Ozarks and Cavern but could also actually tour the "Shepherd of the Hills Country," as the region came to be known. This region could be accessed by rail or, later, automobile, and there were soon regularly scheduled bus or taxi tours of the sights and sites of Wright's story. Marvel Cave, a tourist attraction for decades by the arrival of the twentieth century, was also readily accessible.

The following is a description of the experience of Kansas City newlyweds who honeymooned in the Shepherd of the Hills Country in July 1915. Note that they were "guided" through an entertainment sequence designed to fulfill their expectation of such:

> *Their Cadillac Roadster could not negotiate the high flood waters in Bates County so, like other tourists, they stored their car and rode the train to Branson. Once there they rode the Sammy Lane tourist boat to Powersite (Dam), enjoyed fishing for a couple of hours, hiked to Forsyth, and took the ferry across the river and walked up the bluff to the Cliff House club. At Powersite,* locals introduced themselves as "hillbillies" and the young urban couple joined in dancing with them and "had no end of fun." [emphasis added]

In a two-week stay, in addition to visiting the Rose O'Neill house (the creator of the Kewpie Doll), the couple visited every locale in the Bell Wright book, had dinner with "Old Matt" and "Aunt Molly," met "Uncle Ike" and toured Marvel Cave. Reportedly, the honeymoon trip was a huge success.

With the exception of meeting the Bell Wright models, the experience, as related in Lynn Morrow's *Shepherd of the Hills Country: Tourism Transforms the Ozarks, 1880s–1930s,* does not sound all that different from that of twenty-first-century tourism in Branson.

The Branson area/Shepherd of the Hills Country was already an established tourist destination by the time Ralph Street began to visualize the damming of the Osage River.

In terms of transportation, organization and promotion, the exterior region had covered its bases. In 1919, for example, the Ozarks Playground Association was formed, and a cohesive, comprehensive promotion campaign was undertaken with an advertisement tagline: "The Land of a Million Smiles."

At the Lake of the Ozarks, development did not accelerate until the late 1940s, and even then the pace was at a crawl.

In pre-lake days, locals of the interior Ozarks found the concept of tourism alien. By all accounts, the population surrounding the Lake of the Ozarks were taken completely by surprise when seven thousand tourists arrived in their midst for the opening day of Bagnell Dam in 1931.

The determining factor in the development of the Lake of the Ozarks was not tourism (although that market was eventually vigorously pursued) but the availability of the shoreline for private ownership, offered as small lots with usually little more than fifty feet of shoreline and property back of about that same distance. And there was little shoreline that was not for sale; a dense, small-lot, permanent (but seasonal) population was the goal of the early developers.

So in both regions, Branson and the Lake of the Ozarks, an urban structure was in place from the beginnings of the post-rural development. In Branson, the urban vortex was defined by the Shepherd of the Hills Country perimeters, and at the Lake of the Ozarks region, the definition was provided by the lake's rambling, over one-thousand-mile shoreline.

In what we are calling the "urbanization" process, once such physical structure is in place, urban components begin to coalesce and develop within it in accordance with the organizing principles of the culture. This is particularly evident when there are no planning or zoning efforts in the area's growth (as was the case in outstate Missouri during the time frame of this narrative).

The kind of development under discussion will usually first organize around proximity—in the case of Branson, for example, tourist entertainment would lead to an attraction called Silver Dollar City, located within the long-established tourist destination Marvel Cave and close by the Shepherd of the Hills sites, as well as the early music theaters of the 1950s. In the Lake of the Ozarks region, Bagnell Dam acted as the original anchor for development, and thus Lee Mace's Ozark Opry

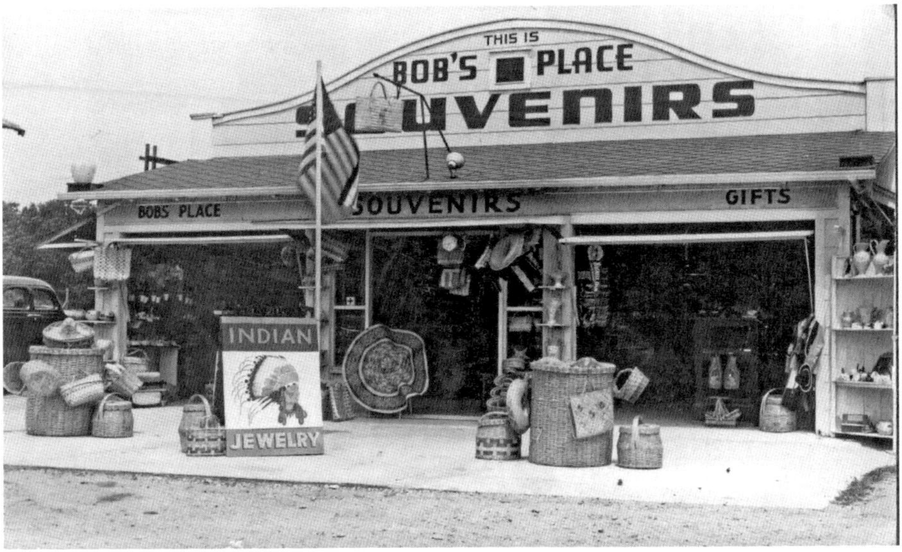

A fine example of an early 1950s souvenir store to serve the curiosity of the Ozark travelers and tourists. *Courtesy of Miller County Missouri Historical Society.*

and other early attractions and enterprises were located in the Lakeside Casino building and "strip" area close by the dam.

Each of the two regions began organizing within an urban structure according to its understanding of commercial demand and its own needs. While there are similar elements in the two subject regions, their approaches to what was to be offered in response to commercial demand were distinct.

At the Lake of the Ozarks, what the locals had learned in interacting with outsiders was that there was a high demand for participatory activities, such as swimming, fishing, boating and the like. In a 2010 interview, Joyce Mace recalled that in the first decade of the Ozark Opry operation, the shows did not start until 9:00 p.m. because "people were out on the lake until then."

On the other hand, in Branson it was understood that the tourist sites and entertainment venues were the destination. As time passed and the "Golden Age" of Branson dawned in the 1980s, this premise became accepted to the point that during the season, music venues staged performances at all hours of the day (starting as early as nine o'clock in the morning) and into the evening.

Chapter 17

THE 5 PERCENT SOLUTION

The three decades between the formation of the Lake of the Ozarks and the early 1960s was a time of very little innovation in services available to visitors or expansion of the perspective the locals had of what the tourist trade consisted of.

With the notable exception of Cyrus Willmore's efforts, the local approach to outsiders visiting the north central (interior) Ozarks from the 1930s through the 1950s was the same as it had been in the pre-lake times, when such visitors were rare and generally in the market for fishing or hiking trips. A number of tourist camps were established between the ends of the Great Depression on to the Korean Police Action years, but these were usually clusters of small cabins with few or no amenities and no provisions for entertainment or often not even much interaction of hosts with guests.

As time passed, larger such operations were established—the best remembered may include Millstone Lodge and Wolf Harbor among others. These maintained basically the same "tourist camp" attitudes as their predecessors. They were just bigger, and some had restaurant facilities and guest lounges, but the assumption was still that the tourists would figure out what to do with themselves out there on the lake or in the woods or wherever they might go off during the day.

When considering the stagnancy of attitude toward opportunity evident in those times, it is important to remember that the region in which the Lake of the Ozarks had suddenly materialized had been considerably isolated for most of its history. Be mindful that the time span from the first surveys in

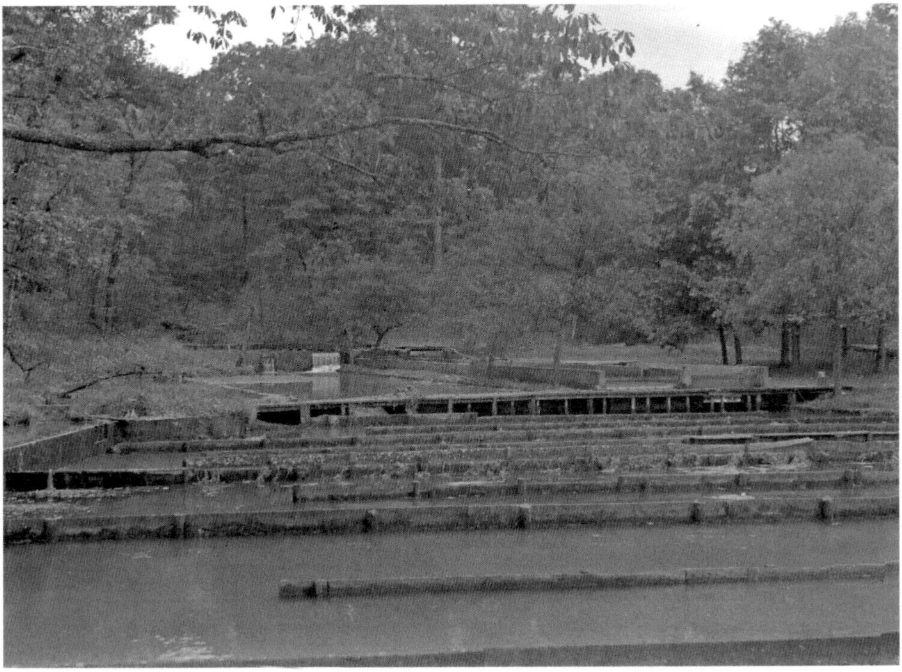

Collins Springs, later known as Troutdale, is home of the farthest north large Ozark springs capable of supporting live trout. It was known as a viable source of water and water power for the mills located along the Gravois. Locals reminisce about the early years of the spring water being guided along its path through wooden sloughs to the area mills. As early as the 1920s, trout were raised in the stream. *Courtesy of Missouri State Capitol Commission, Missouri State Archives.*

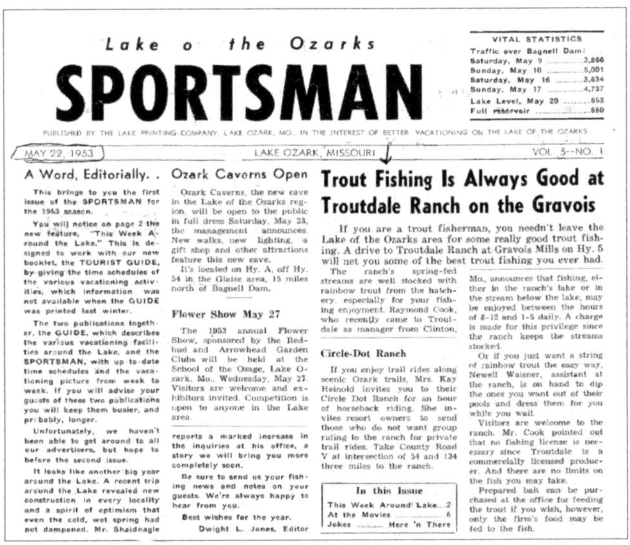

Lake o the Ozarks

SPORTSMAN

VITAL STATISTICS	
Traffic over Bagnell Dam:	
Saturday, May 9	3,866
Sunday, May 10	5,001
Saturday, May 16	3,634
Sunday, May 17	4,737
Lake Level, May 20	653
Full reservoir	660

PUBLISHED BY THE LAKE PRINTING COMPANY, LAKE OZARK, MO., IN THE INTEREST OF BETTER VACATIONING ON THE LAKE OF THE OZARKS

MAY 22, 1953 — LAKE OZARK, MISSOURI — VOL. 5--NO. 1

A Word, Editorially. .

This brings to you the first issue of the SPORTSMAN for the 1953 season.

You will notice on page 2 the new feature, "This Week Around the Lake." This is designed to work with our new booklet, the TOURIST GUIDE, by giving the time schedules of the various vacationing activities, which information was not available when the GUIDE was printed last winter.

The two publications together, the GUIDE, which describes the various vacationing facilities around the Lake, and the SPORTSMAN, with up-to-date time schedules and the vacationing picture from week to week. If you will advise your guests of these two publications you will keep them busier, and probably, longer.

Unfortunately, we haven't been able to get around to all our advertisers, but hope to before the second issue.

It looks like another big year around the Lake. A recent trip around the Lake revealed new construction in every locality and a spirit of optimism that even the cold, wet spring had not dampened. Mr. Shaidnagle reports a marked increase in the inquiries at his office, a story we will bring you more completely soon.

Be sure to send us your fishing news and notes on your guests. We're always happy to hear from you.

Best wishes for the year.

Dwight L. Jones, Editor

Ozark Caverns Open

Ozark Caverns, the new cave in the Lake of the Ozarks region, will be open to the public in full dress Saturday, May 23, the management announces. New walks, new lighting, a gift shop and other attractions feature this new cave.

It's located on Hy. A, off Hy. 54 in the Glaize area, 15 miles north of Bagnell Dam.

Flower Show May 27

The 1953 annual Flower Show, sponsored by the Redbud and Arrowhead Garden Clubs will be held at the School of the Osage, Lake Ozark, Mo., Wednesday, May 27. Visitors are welcome and exhibitors invited. Competition is open to anyone in the Lake area.

Trout Fishing Is Always Good at Troutdale Ranch on the Gravois

If you are a trout fisherman, you needn't leave the Lake of the Ozarks area for some really good trout fishing. A drive to Troutdale Ranch at Gravois Mills on Hy. 5 will net you some of the best trout fishing you ever had.

The ranch's spring-fed streams are well stocked with rainbow trout from the hatchery, especially for your fishing enjoyment. Raymond Cook, who recently came to Troutdale as manager from Clinton, Mo., announces that fishing, either in the ranch's lake or in the stream below the lake, may be enjoyed between the hours of 8-12 and 1-5 daily. A charge is made for this privilege since the ranch keeps the streams stocked.

Or if you just want a string of rainbow trout the easy way, Newell Waisner, assistant at the ranch, is on hand to dip the ones you want out of their pools and dress them for you while you wait.

Visitors are welcome to the ranch. Mr. Cook pointed out that no fishing license is necessary since Troutdale is a commercially licensed producer. And there are no limits on the fish you may take.

Prepared bait can be purchased at the office for feeding the trout if you wish, however, only the firm's food may be fed to the fish.

Circle-Dot Ranch

If you enjoy trail rides along scenic Ozark trails, Mrs. Kay Heinold invites you to their Circle Dot Ranch for an hour of horseback riding. She invites resort owners to send those who do not want group riding to the ranch for private trail rides. Take County Road V at intersection of 54 and 134 three miles to the ranch.

In this Issue

This Week Around Lake ... 2
At the Movies ... 6
Jokes ... Here 'n There

Troutdale's 1953 fishing season is highlighted in this May 22, 1953 news article from the *Lake of the Ozarks Sportsman*. One could fish for his own trout or purchase fresh live trout to take with him. No license was required, and there was no limit on the number of fish taken. *Author's private collection (KVL).*

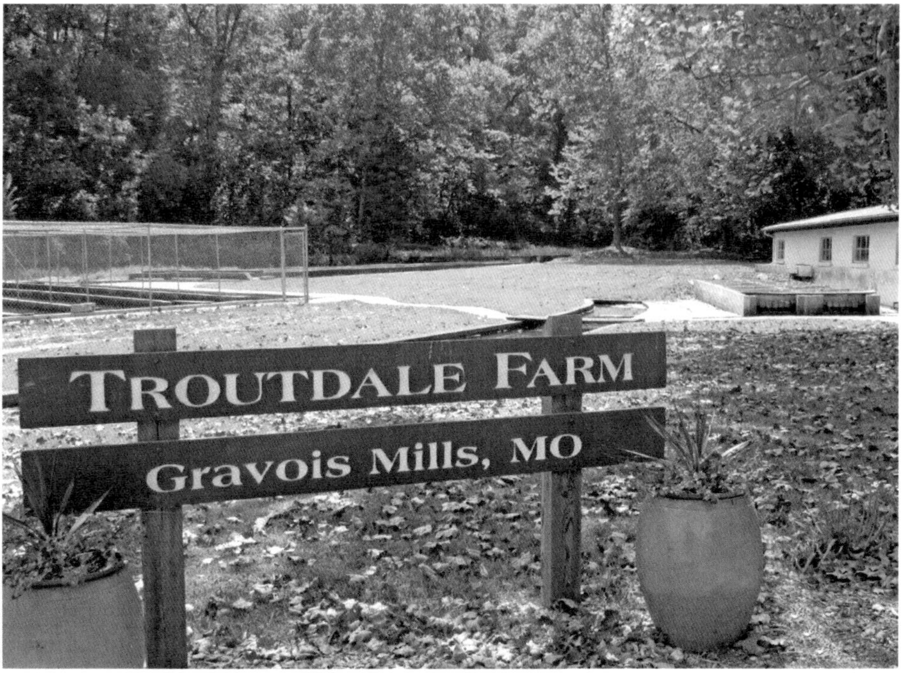

Troutdale continues operation in the twenty-first century as an aqua farming operation, providing fresh trout to Midwest restaurants and private individuals. One can also tour the trout farm while enjoying the quiet, serene valley and the abundant wildlife. *Author's private collection (KVL).*

the mid-1920s until completion of the dam's construction spanned less than a decade. And the creation of the lake was followed by extended periods of indifferent ownership of the shoreline by Union Electric.

A fairly significant segment of the local population had never expected Bagnell Dam to be successfully constructed—ever—and the tourists coming on the heels of the completion of the dam were completely unanticipated.

It was St. Louis native Cyrus Crane Willmore—and a younger generation of the locals following his lead—who understood that whatever the number of Depression-era, war-wearied visitors and tourists showing up on the shores of the new electric lake, many would have to be *taught* how to vacation in this Ozarks wonderland.

But progress in promotion of the Lake of the Ozarks as a vacation and recreation destination was nonetheless close to three decades in gathering any significant momentum. Such momentum may have accelerated sooner had it not been for Willmore's untimely death in 1949. As it was, Al Elam and others have stated that it was well into the 1950s and indeed the 1960s

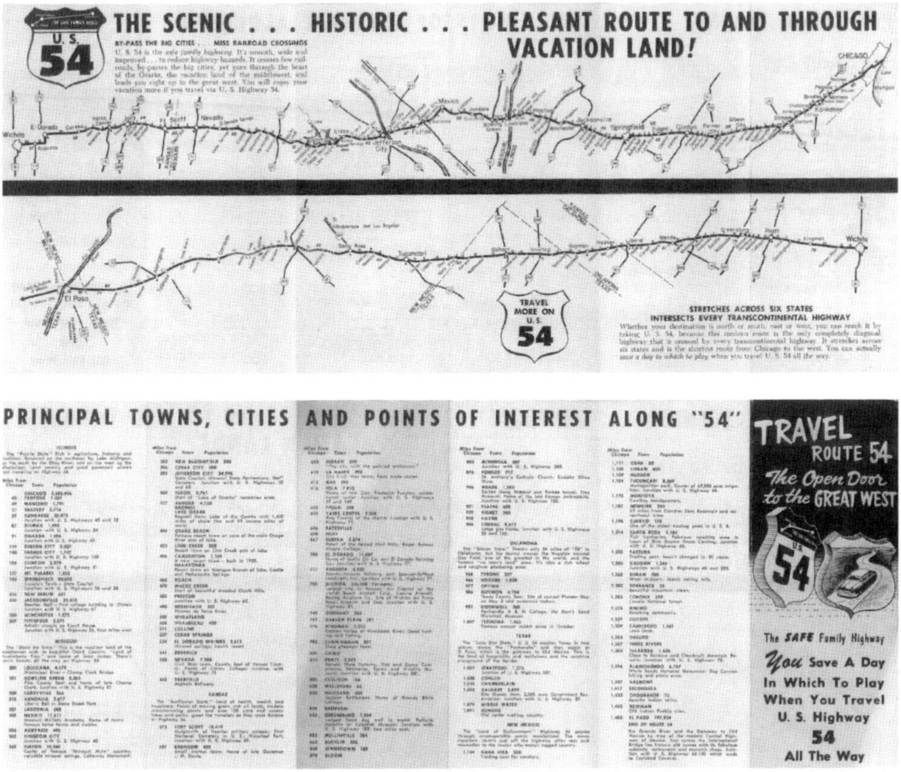

An early 1950s promotion for U.S. 54 tells travelers to "Travel Route 54—The Open Door to the GREAT WEST." It lists all the towns, along with their points of interest, and population of each town. *Author's private collection (KVL).*

before the lake began to project an image beyond the outdoorsy, bare-bones cabin and camp look of the 1930s.

What was evident was the near complete lack of understanding of a new tourist economy. A phrase of the time that is most telling is "camp eats"—meaning, apparently, groceries that could be used when camping out or when staying at the early motel-type operations known as "tourist camps." This was what the "old lake" locals thought people came to the lake to do.

A great deal of ink was also expended on announcements of the availability of "5 percent beer." The strength of brew was apparently considered a major marketing point. The tale therein is straightforward and dates from the Prohibition era. In 1933, the Volstead Act was amended to allow the sale of beer with no more than 3.2 percent alcohol content (the Blaine Act), and shortly thereafter, Volstead as a whole was repealed. Prohibition was over.

In any case, the travel originations of many of the tourists—notably Kansans—had remained "dry" even after the Volstead Act and the Eighteenth Amendment had been repealed. Between the lingering effects of the Blaine Act and "dry" constituencies in the region, it is probable tourists and visitors to the Ozarks might have often inquired about the potency of the locally proffered beer and thereby sparked the trumpeting of the stronger brew in ads.

But, with the exception of Lee Mace, few 1950s operators in the lake area seemed to have any grasp on tourism marketing and promotion whatsoever.

Immediately with the dawning of the 1960s though, an unforeshadowed transformation occurred, effected from three distinct directions—first, the emergence of a band of young entrepreneurs native to the region; next, the arrival of wealthy property developers and promoters who came not as visiting players or country squires but as heavily invested stakeholders with overarching vision for the future of the lake and the will to make that vision a reality; and simultaneously, the growing establishment of nationally franchised lodging and dining chain operations alongside the old lake-style tourist camps and diners.

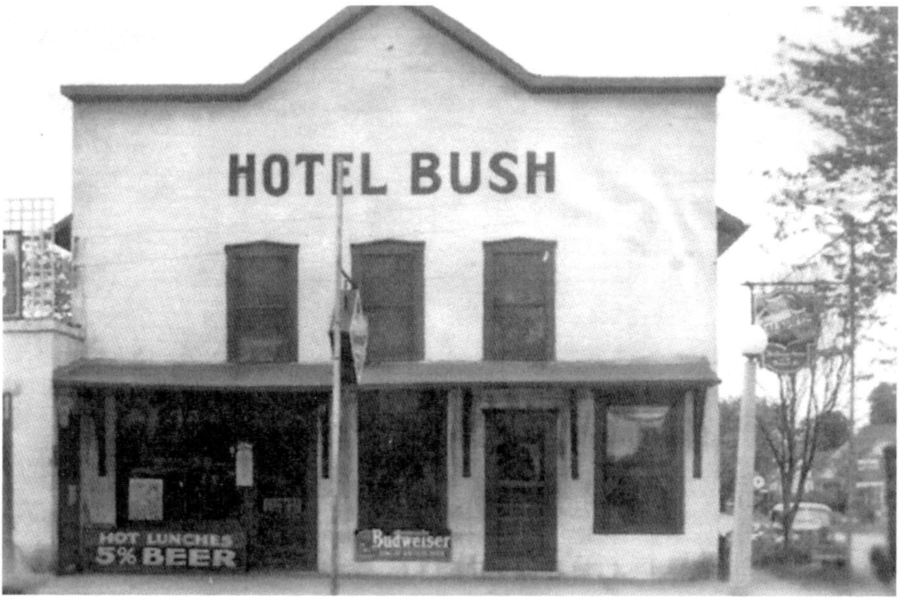

This photo catches the Bush Hotel on the south side of the Versailles square. Note the "5% Beer" signs for Budweiser and Falstaff. The lake visitors enjoyed the local availability of 5 percent beer. If one was coming to the west side of the lake from the Kansas City area and western Missouri, they would drive through downtown Versailles and right past these businesses. *Courtesy of Morgan County Historical Society.*

Certainly foremost in the cadre of youthful entrepreneurs who would shape the future of the Lake of the Ozarks was Lee Mace. By the early 1960s, Lee Mace's Ozark Opry was probably the highest-profile business and tourist attraction in the region. Mace was a tireless promoter of lake tourism and investment.

Bill "Goofer" Atterberry, the Ozark Opry's beloved country comedian, once observed that when the troupe was on tour, "we always handed out brochures about the lake, and Lee ended most shows saying, 'We came to see you, now y'all come to see us.'"

From near the beginnings of Lee Mace's Ozark Opry, short-lived competitors had opened on the dam "strip" (the continuation of the dam-top highway that featured various tourist-oriented businesses) or nearby, trying to lure tourist audiences with the promise of country music and even "Nashville Stars." In the 1950s and 1960s, most city folk tourists were completely unfamiliar with country music, had no idea what a "Nashville Star" was and had little interest in finding out.

What is perhaps strange is that Lee never made any attempt to disguise his formula for success—dress the cast up as what the tourist trade would think hillbillies would look like and then play mostly traditional-style fiddle and banjo country music—the kind of music that sounded familiar to most Americans even when they couldn't put a name to it.

But until the 1970s, when Nashville-style country-pop music had penetrated to urban audiences like those who vacationed at the lake, opening a "country" music show in proximity of the Ozark Opry was a sure way to lose money.

But the Ozark Opry was also an anchor for Lee and Joyce Mace's other entrepreneurial efforts, which accelerated in the 1960s. Joining with other young businesspeople from the area, most in their thirties or early forties, the Maces moved to ratchet up the lake's profile and interests. These individuals were scions of the old Ozark oligarchy and were "true locals." Some of their ancestors had settled in the north central Ozarks on the heels of Daniel Boone's land deal with Spain.

James "Jim" Franklin Sr.'s story of his ancestors' 1832 arrival in what would become Camden County is perhaps relatively typical of the group. Franklin's three times great-grandfather was Isaac "Ike" Garrison, born in 1732 and a soldier with Washington's army at Valley Forge. In 1832, Ike Garrison came to Missouri with his family, crossing the Mississippi at Cairo, Illinois (pronounced "Kae-roe"). "Grandpa" Ike was seated in a chair on the top of a wagon for the crossing and, it would seem predictably, toppled from that perch into the river. Franklin maintained his ancestor was "the only one-hundred-year-old to ever swim across the Mississippi."

Jim Franklin Sr. and Carl Williams pursued careers following familial leads. Franklin's grandfather "Swede Charley" Anderson had been a prominent banker in the area in the early twentieth century, and Carl Williams's family had established a grocery during the years of the Great Depression, operating it successfully throughout the hard times.

Franklin, Williams and Mace would act with Al Elam and other members of the local oligarchy to organize much of the successful commercial culture that centered on the lake's east side.

Most significantly, in the early 1960s, Franklin, Mace and Williams, with others, founded a financial institution, the Bank of the Lake of the Ozarks, and from that base, they soon individually and with partners owned much of the property in the area and jointly exercised considerable control over regional affairs.

Chapter 18

IMPORTING THE ELSEWHERE

The 1960s and 1970s witnessed "new lake" attempts to attract tourist and vacationer dollars at the Lake of the Ozarks, many of which were characterized by gimmickry. The inability to understand the culture and expectations of city folk who arrived seasonally or to accept the drawing power of Ozarks (hillbilly) imagery by most of the promoters and merchants of the area created the perception of a need to import or create novelty entertainment venues and attractions.

The novelty approach is perhaps best represented by the Aquarama underwater show, which presented "The world's most beautiful and novel underwater show! Beautiful girls that live like fish! Daring Aqualads in the monster fight! The musical underwater revue for young and old."

The show was pretty much as it sounds: young people swimming underwater in a gigantic tank with a fifty-foot plate-glass front, doing stunts in flesh-colored bodysuits and a variety of swimwear. The Aquarama, patterned on a similar show in Weeki Wachee, Florida, ran from 1964 to 1973 in Osage Beach.

Next to Lee Mace's Ozark Opry, the most frequently recollected and perhaps most popular of the early tourist attractions is one that showcased exotic reptiles and animals but had little to do with the Ozarks. There was also a Dogpatch, a retail operation established in the late 1940s and extant into the twenty-first century. The marketing message was based on a popular twentieth-century cartoon series about a community of hillbillies who lived in Kentucky—the theme, however, could have applied to any mountainous place from Arkansas to West Virginia.

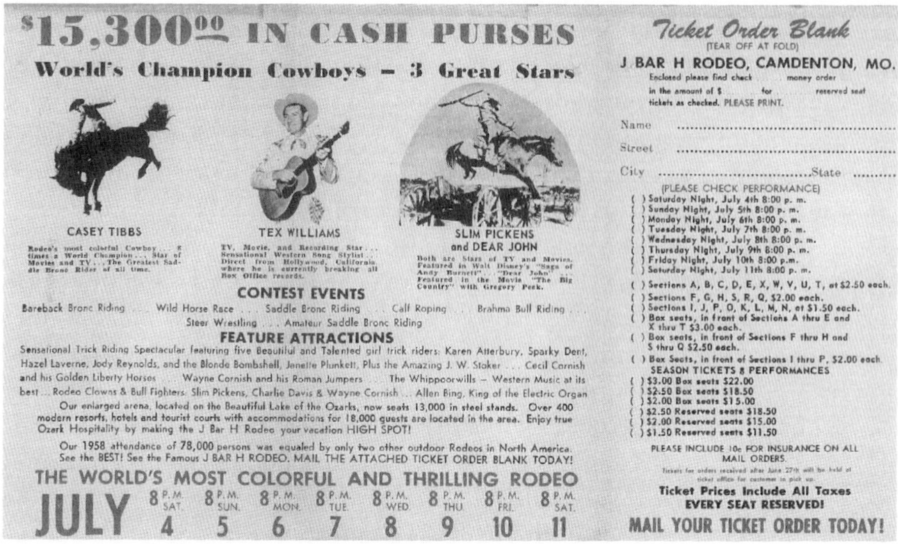

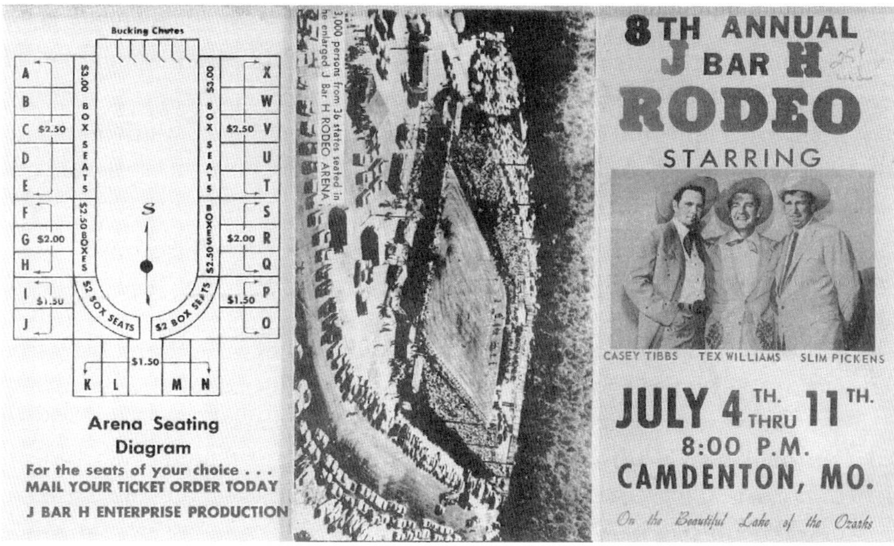

This page: This 1959 J Bar H Rodeo pamphlet provides information for an annual major entertainment venue at the lake in the 1950s and 1960s. *Author's private collection (KVL).*

Opposite: A postcard trumpeting the entertaining adventures on the Larry Don Ozark Sunset Cruise. Visitors could enjoy a dance band and a well-stocked snack and set-up bar, along with a beautiful view. Through the many years, thousands of people enjoyed this great venture on the beautiful Lake of the Ozarks. The excursion boats out of the Loc-Wood boat dock, located on the east side of Bagnell Dam, were tourist mainstays for many years. *Author's private collection (KVL).*

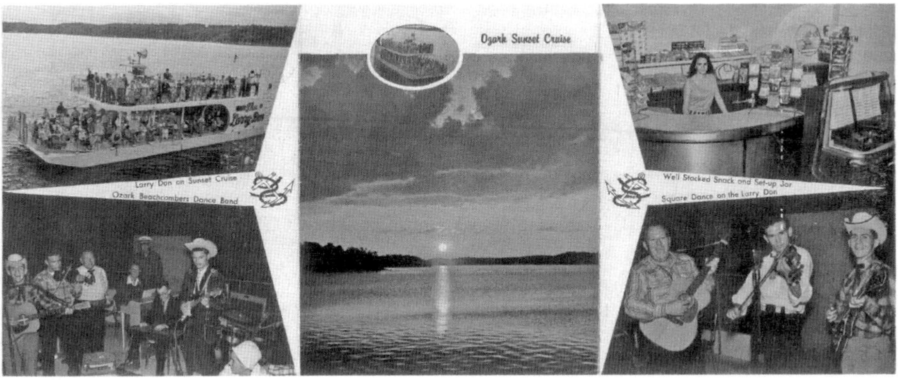

So the conventional wisdom of Lake of the Ozarks marketing was set—the "brand" might reference the lake, but the look and feel of the brand would be of "elsewhere." The look of "elsewhere" in the form of franchised lodging and dining operations had arrived and settled in at the lake by the 1960s.

In franchising, a proven business format is "cloned" through the establishment of uniform standards and specifications for operation, which are then joined to the chain store benefits of mass purchasing and leveraged promotion funding. The clone operations are then licensed to others, forming a franchised network. What this uniformity of operation and leveraging of purchasing power translates to for a franchise operation is the ability to access group discounts for product and marketing costs plus the ability to offer consumers the assurance of a familiar experience and standard of service at any of the franchised outlets. To emphasize this, the franchised outlets are generally required to look like all the other outlets of the network.

So when a Howard Johnson's Motor Lodge and Restaurant opened in Osage Beach in the mid-1960s, many tourists and visitors immediately recognized the brand, the signs and indicia and knew what to expect when they patronized the venue because they had the same experience at a Howard Johnson's elsewhere.

This was much different from the tourist camp and local diner experience in which first visits were almost always a gamble on the delivery of product or service.

Simultaneous with the invasion of the franchised operators came another equally determined "elsewhere" branding: the construction of two luxury resorts that opened during the 1960s, Tan-Tar-A and the Lodge of the Four Seasons, both of which remain in operation to this day.

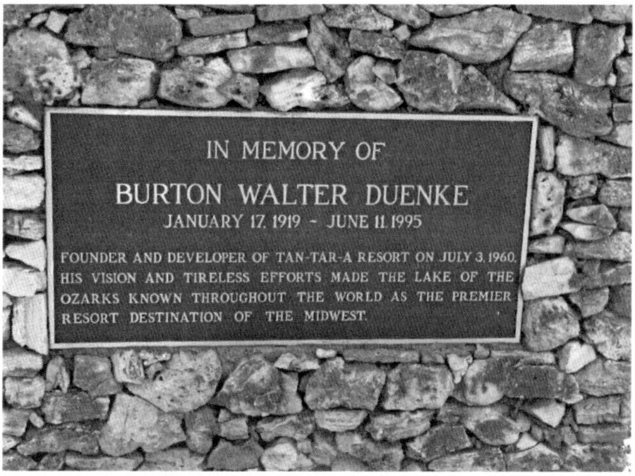

Burton Duenke is memorialized as an important figure in expanding the lake-area identity as a national and international tourist destination. He developed the Tan-Tar-A resort as a destination alternative to the Ozark-style entertainment. *Author's private collection (DWP).*

Both resorts owed their existence to the determination of St. Louis millionaires Burton Duenke and Harold Koplar. Unlike the city operatives of pre-dam days and the UE era, this pair had a vision for the lake as a commercial fulcrum, and both were prepared to invest in that vision to the point of do or die.

The locals marveled at the sight of Duenke's spectacular Oriental-themed Tan-Tar-A and at Koplar's opulent spread with its money-sounding name and European style.

As if to erase any doubt as to their vision for the Lake of the Ozarks as an upper-end destination, both the Duenke and Koplar operations moved to establish fine dining and eventually other "elsewhere" features, such as professionally designed regulation golf courses and expensive "spa" centers as part of their resorts.

Local restaurateur and historian Joseph Boer described the transition thusly:

> *Elegant dining was introduced by Burton Duenke when he opened Der Krug at Tan-Tar-A. He hired wait staff* [sic] *and chefs from New Orleans and the Caribbean Islands. They wore tuxedos, and guests too, were required to dress appropriately…Harold Koplar at the Four Seasons offered fine dining in the Ozarks in his Toledo Room. His wait staff also wore tuxedos, and strolling violinists and sometimes jugglers were engaged. Flaming after-dinner drinks and marvelous dining options were his style.*[1]

Boer, himself a well-known figure in lake lore who has founded popular upscale restaurants in the area, also noted that jazz greats like Stan Kenton were imported to play the new luxury resorts.

So it was that significant numbers of primary movers at the modern Lake of the Ozarks decided that the marketing of the lake would be unlike any previous Ozarks tourism promotion (both that of the interior and exterior). The allure of the lake, the luxury operators felt, would best be founded in similarity to more splendored or exotic travel and vacation experiences—the Caribbean, the French Quarter, even the far-away Orient and South Pacific. In addition to the Oriental-themed architecture and gardens at Tan-Tar-A, there was a tiki-themed resort, the Mai Tai, which operated contemporaneously with the construction of the new luxury lodges.

This "elsewhere" approach to marketing the lake completely ignored the regional culture. This ignorance was not lost on the true locals and indeed may have exacerbated the resentment that smoldered with the generations of the region's pre-lake populace.

But for the "elsewhere entrepreneurs" of that day, there were more immediate challenges to importing "elsewhere" into the Ozark culture of the region. One of the more daunting was the prohibition of liquor sales by the drink.

The old Ozark ordinaries were generally of two sorts, the roadhouses and the set-up operations. The roadhouses were beer joint dance halls. The more sophisticated operations seldom offered beer but rather provided "set-up" service. Patrons brought their own booze with them and paid the establishment a somewhat inflated fee for ice, glass and mixer.

However, venturing into an Ozarks roadhouse required the kind of adventurous spirit that most tourists did not pack, and finding oneself in a "set-up" room without the requisite bottle was a disappointment to the uninformed visitor. More to the point, the lack of liquor by the drink was a major obstacle to attracting large convention and conference business to the new lake's luxury and franchised resort destinations.

Local lore has it that the solution to the liquor-by-the-drink dilemma was provided in 1970 when Missouri governor Warren E. Hearnes had been elected president of the National Governors Association (NGA). Not one to miss an opportunity, and working with Missouri Hospitality industry figures—notably the Lodge of the Four Seasons owner, Harold Koplar—Hearnes succeeded in pushing through a change in the liquor laws, which allowed single servings of alcohol and, to do one better, arranged for the NGA convention to be convened in 1970 at one of the new lake luxury resorts: the Lodge of the Four Seasons.

The Lake of the Ozarks' "elsewhere" branding had taken a giant leap forward, as evidenced by the construction of an airport in the Lake of the

Ozarks State Park specifically for the purpose of flying in the NGA attendees for their liquor by the drink convention. The airport was greeted somewhat breathlessly by local business leaders, with one Lake Booster bragging that it could land "practically any commercial airplane."[2]

Chapter 19

A LAND FOR ALL SEASONS

Foreshadowing the 1970s multiplication of Osage Beach music shows (more than a dozen opened during this era) was the improbably successful—at the time—stage show in the Wild Times Saloon at the Lodge of the Four Seasons starting in the mid-1960s. The featured entertainer was Monte Davidson and the Wild Bunch. Davidson (aka "Monte D.") opened the show riding through the audience on Gomer, a male bovine Davidson once described as "a worn-out rodeo bull."

Speaking in 2014, Monte Davidson credited the success of his Wild Times show with a straightforward analysis: "It appealed to both the mountain people and the sophisticates—so everybody could enjoy it." It should be noted that by the time he opened at the Lodge of the Four Seasons, Monte D. was already an entertainer with a national following and reputation.[1]

The aspect of improbability of such a show at the Lake of the Ozarks in the 1960s arises from the fact that the entrepreneur hotelier who hired Monte D. and his band and bull was Harold Koplar, who owned and operated the Chase Park Plaza in St. Louis and who successfully developed one of the first luxury resorts at the Lake of the Ozarks. (Another upscale resort, Tan-Tar-A, opened a few years earlier than the Lodge of the Four Seasons.)

By all accounts, Koplar—known to friends and senior employees by his initials, HK—was a charming, energetic multimillionaire who was given to impulse action and was blessed, most of the time, with overarching vision and an ability to make that vision work.

Koplar did not, however, seem to have the "common touch" that had greased the skids for Cyrus Willmore in his relations with the true locals of the Ozarks region where he was to venture. HK's biographer, Candace O'Connor, described Koplar's people skills thusly: "Harold Koplar would stop by the [Chase Park Plaza] kitchens before a banquet to see how things were going—say a kind word, take a personal interest in their lives. Yet he was not at all interested in the nitty-gritty details, including the hotel's balance sheet. He was the visionary, the creator, and he left the day-to-day operations to his trusted lieutenants."

The groundbreaking for the Lodge of Four Seasons can be described as the beginning of the end of the "old lake" era. The initial one-hundred-acre purchase of land in Horseshoe Bend represented the approaching liquidation of the last Ozarks holdings of Cyrus Crane Willmore's heirs, and the advent of the two luxury resorts signaled a "new" lake both of image and substance.

But in the early 1960s Ozarks that HK ventured into, the "new" lake was only a dim silhouette against a backdrop of treacherous mud roads, mountains thick with brittle second-growth forest and rock-strewn fields surrounding a sprawling body of water that only made sense to the electric company that had caused it to be.

O'Connor wrote, "For years, the Lake remained a sleepy backwater that changed little, except for a couple of modest sized lodges and Burton Duenke's 'Tan-Tar-A' resort, opened in 1960. Jed Duncan, later a landscaper for Harold Koplar, recalled the lakeside land that would become the site of Koplar's Lodge. 'There was nothing here but a log barn and pasture. Route HH was a rough gravel road. I worked this property with my dad and uncle when I was 12 years old, cutting tree sprouts out of the field for Mr. Willmore's 2,000 head of cattle,' he said. 'The land was worth little especially to locals.'"

A celebrity world-class hotelier and media mogul (KPLR-TV), Koplar suddenly found himself dealing with the prideful, stubborn true locals of the Ozarks. O'Connor explains:

> *On site, Koplar discovered he was facing a culture with a completely different work ethic. There was a kind of manana atmosphere, said Tom Schultz, former director of the Lake of the Ozarks Association. "People were not used to working the way they did in the cities. Down there, hell, they'd drop work in the afternoon and go fishing if the crappie were hitting. In March, below the dam they would snag for catfish, and in hunting*

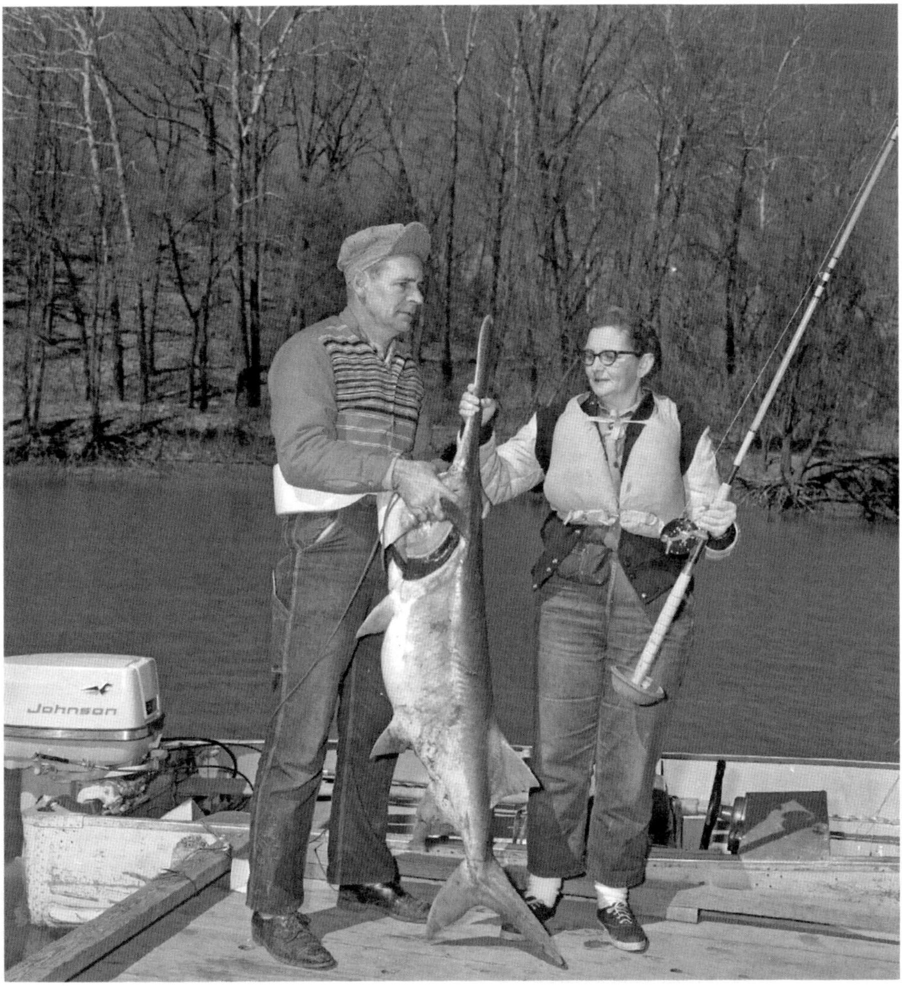

This couple is enjoying a successful "snag" of a nice paddlefish on the Osage River. This was a traditional experience found only in the Ozarks and was very representative of the era. *Courtesy of Missouri State Capitol Commission, Missouri State Archives.*

> *season, they were out hunting for deer..." There were also local politics to contend with: the small family resorts were jealous of the large...resorts; the two sides of the Lake were at odds with one another. "And there was no sense of promoting the Lake as a destination," added Schultz, "until Harold Koplar came along."*[2]

There was opposition lurking at every turn, and every effort was met with, at best, the Ozarks brand of passive aggression and, at worst, the

Ozarks brand of flat-out aggression. For example, a Japanese landscape designer Koplar had imported from Hollywood was set upon by locals and severely beaten.

HK had planned a soft grand opening with other celebrity hoteliers, politicians and entertainers in attendance at a gala formal feast and fêté event. But he got no cooperation from any quarter. O'Connor elaborates:

> *Guests arrived at the local airport in a rainstorm and, when they got to the Lodge, had to navigate six inches of mud in the unpaved driveway…that afternoon workmen were still laying carpet in the lobby.*
>
> *"There was some good ol' boy from the Ozarks working away in a nice, deliberate fashion," recalled corporate attorney Dempster Holland. "And Harold went up to him and said 'You've got to finish that carpet by six o'clock.' The guy looked up at him and said 'Mr. Koplar, I don't got to do* nothing,*' laid down his tools and walked out."*

(Note: the rural work style outlined by James Wise in our note to Chapter 14 explains this incident).

The Chase Park Plaza managers incorrectly—but understandably—assigned a lack of work ethic to the troublesome local labor. Ozarkers were accustomed to hard work (and, although the managers may have thought otherwise, the fishing and hunting breaks were probably not for sport). What did not work was the management style the city men projected, which was the modern, efficiency-expert, near-military, chain-of-command model—an urban style.

In many Ozark enterprises of that time, the only difference in the workplace between managers and workers were their duties—bosses didn't, as a rule, act like "bosses." Outside of the workplace, there were no distinctions in status at all, and the managers came out to the homes of the workers for regular pig pickins (hog roasts) and other get-togethers and vice versa.

Cy Willmore mimicked the Ozark business management style. He would, for example, often invite workers to ride around the lake property with him in his pickup truck and talk with them about his plans as he would with a friend.

Although he was hardwired into the Hollywood and Las Vegas entertainment world, HK wisely chose to hire help in booking performers for the lodge dining and entertainment venues.

Enter Monte Davidson and his bull, Gomer. Davidson was a country-western entertainer made good, and he played Las Vegas regularly and

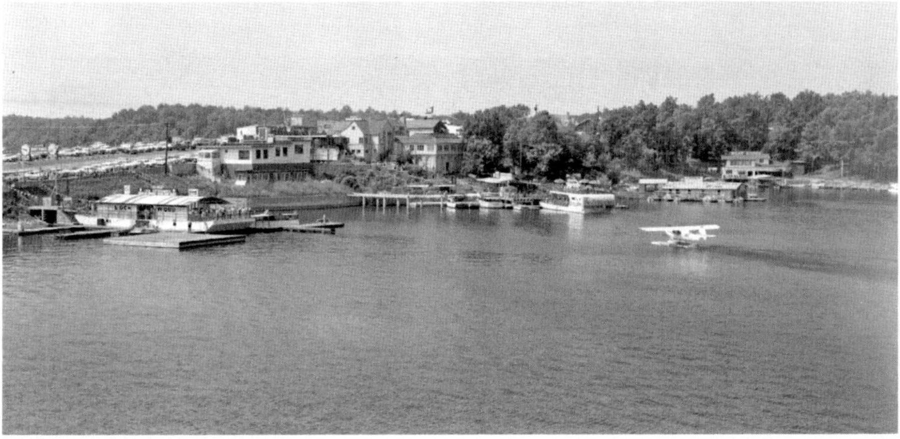

This 1950s-era photo shows the high level of activity on the west side of Bagnell Dam, known as the strip. On the left side of the photo, there is the full parking lot. Photo left center shows the Loc-Wood boat docks for multiple excursion rides and people lined up for the next trip. At the center is the excursion boat *Larry Don*, full of sightseers leaving for their cruise and a sea plane arriving to take the next group for the awesome aerial view of the lake. *Courtesy of Missouri State Capitol Commission, Missouri State Archives.*

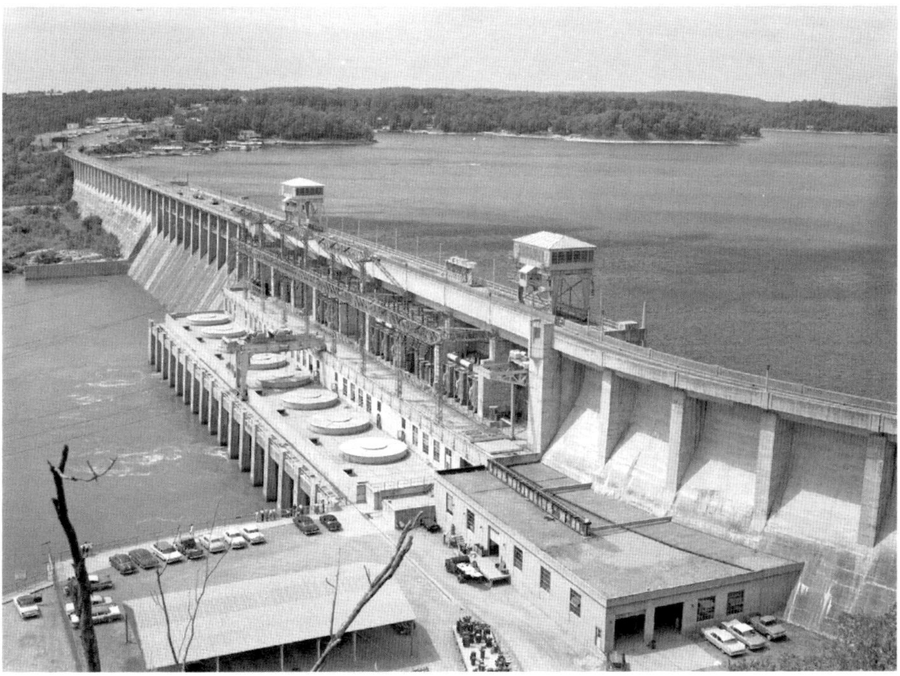

This 1950s-era photo shows the high level of development activity on the west side of Bagnell Dam. *Courtesy of Missouri State Capitol Commission, Missouri State Archives.*

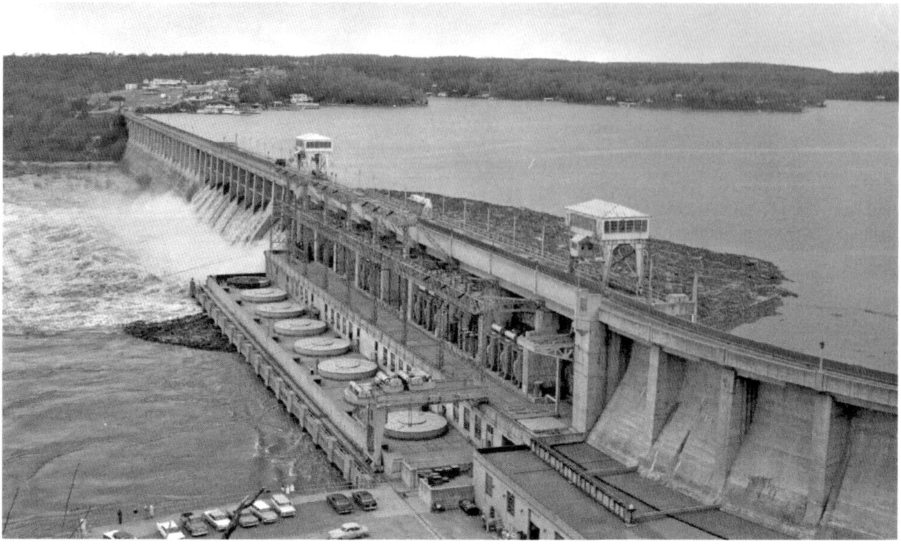

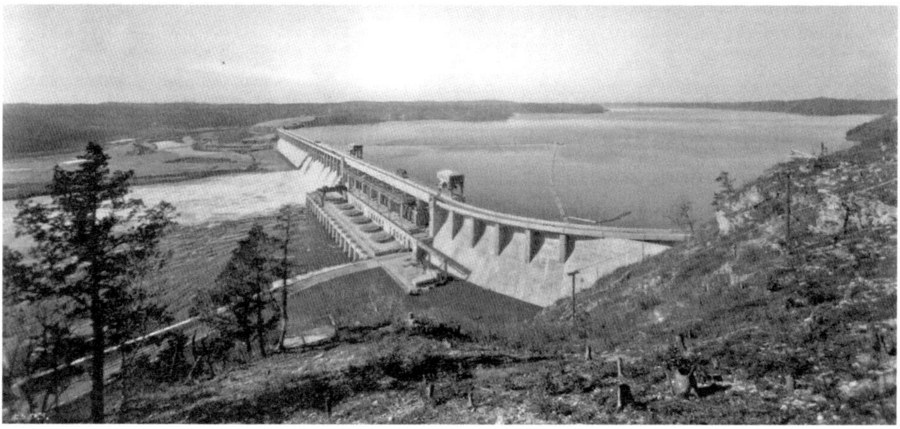

This page, top: Sometimes there was a lot of water. This early 1960s photo shows Bagnell Dam with the flood gates open. This would be before Truman Dam was constructed upstream on the Osage River. Truman Dam was completed in 1979. *Courtesy of Missouri State Capitol Commission, Missouri State Archives.*

This page, bottom: This early photo shows the area on the west side of the dam before commercial development began. Also note the high water with open flood gates. *Courtesy of Missouri State Capitol Commission, Missouri State Archives.*

Opposite, top: This July 27, 1931 Union Electric photo was taken at the completion of the dam construction project. *Courtesy of Missouri State Capitol Commission, Missouri State Archives.*

Opposite, bottom: This August 31, 1931 Union Electric photo was taken a month after the completion of the dam construction project. *Courtesy of Missouri State Capitol Commission, Missouri State Archives.*

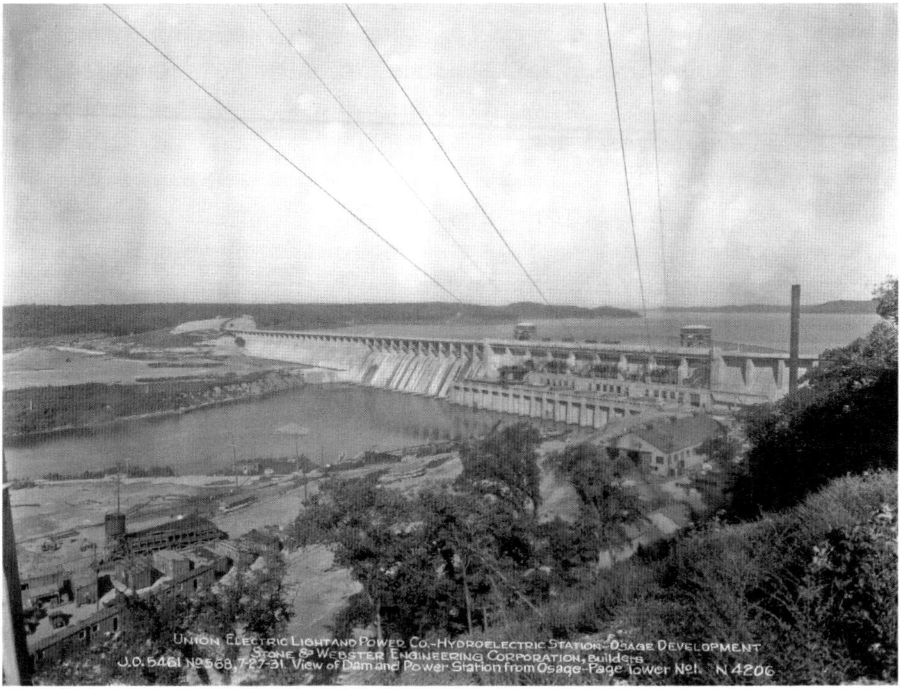
Union Electric Light and Power Co.-Hydroelectric Station-Osage Development
Stone & Webster Engineering Corporation, Builders
J.O. 5461 № 568, 7-27-31. View of Dam and Power Station from Osage-Page Tower № 1. N 4206

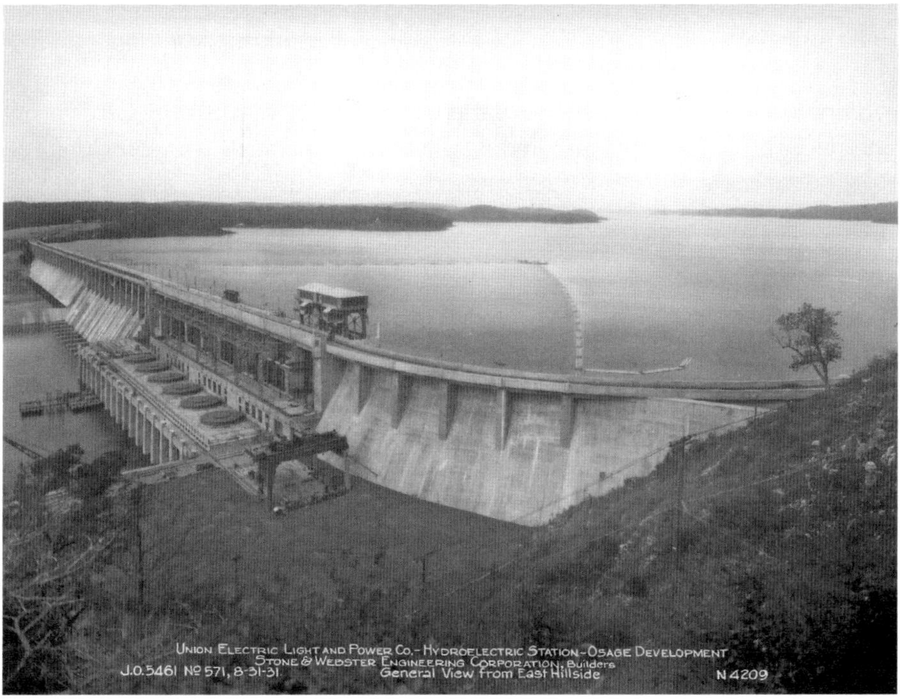
Union Electric Light and Power Co.-Hydroelectric Station-Osage Development
Stone & Webster Engineering Corporation, Builders
J.O. 5461 № 571, 8-31-31. General View from East Hillside N 4209

toured widely. Besides his bull, Davidson was famous for wearing a western-style suit that lighted up and flashed. It is said this was the inspiration for the lighted suit Robert Redford wore in the 1979 movie *The Electric Horseman*.

Davidson credited his lengthy success in show business, however, to the 1980 film *Urban Cowboy*. At ready, Monte D. said he just rode the movie's wave, immediately booking into venues like Mickey Gilley's and frequently touring throughout the decade.

Koplar consulted with Monte on what acts to book at the lodge, recognizing that Davidson had a better handle on what Osage Beach entertainment needed to encompass than he.

One particular 1970s booking is telling. At Monte's advice, Koplar booked at the Wild Times Saloon the popular country star Merle Haggard. The night of the show, HK wanted to do the introduction, and Monte acquiesced, with the result being that Merle Haggard was introduced as "Melvin" Haggard. Country music, while by then prominently featured at the lake, clearly had not yet made its way into the Chase Park Plaza booking rolodex.

In 1970, Harold Koplar acquired vast tracts of additional acres on Horseshoe and Shawnee Bends that were still owned by the Willmore family and set about selling to other city folks, which over the decades has contributed considerably to the urbanization and commercial opportunities that soon attached to the Osage Beach area.

Harold Koplar and the Koplar family made the Lodge of the Four Seasons a success that today is considered, along with Tan-Tar-A, an iconic Lake of the Ozarks institution. HK died at the age of seventy in 1985.

Chapter 20

GOING VERTICAL

By the mid-1980s, the Great Depression and World War II/Korean "Police Action" generations had entered or approached retirement, and their children, the baby boomers, were not far behind. As their pension years loomed, many members of the post–World War II generations who had vacationed or toured the lake during summers throughout their adult lives began eyeing the region as a retirement destination. Their lake shelters of choice, though, were not to be the traditional small lot cabins that had for decades thicketed the shore line nor the emerging "new lake" million-dollar lakeside mansions that had begun to materialize in somewhat improbable numbers but rather full-service, common-area condominium complexes with swimming pools, recreational facilities and attached marinas for the oceangoing vessels many of the new lake residents favored.

Resentment of the seasonal and, more recently, year-round outsiders among the true locals had slowly smoldered and crackled from the first days of the lake. The high-handed displacement of the population of what became the lake bed with the dam flood and the not infrequent Pistol Club and "party cove" sort of behavior sometimes on display during vacation seasons were bedrock of a constant sense of civic and cultural annoyance.

From the latter decades of the twentieth century into the twenty-first, high-rise condominium projects characterized construction along the lake's broader channels—in particular, on the main channel and Osage Beach area.

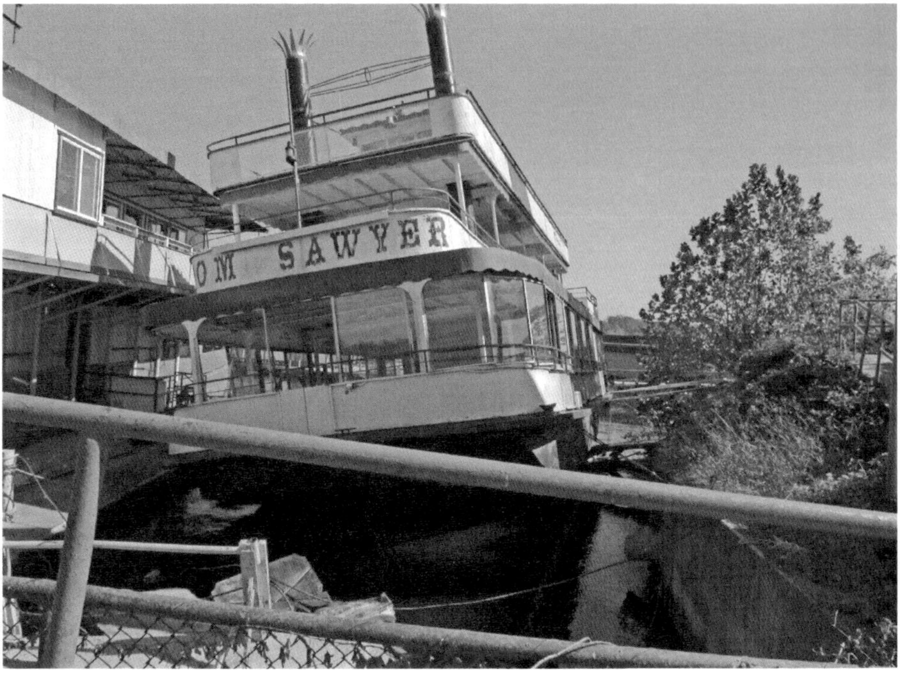

Some entertainment venues don't survive. The lake had many entertainment venues at "the strip" on the west side of Bagnell Dam. One such area was the Loc-Wood excursion boats and sea plane rides. These have become memories. This photo of excursion boat *Tom Sawyer* in dry-dock is a remnant of those fond memories. *Author's private collection (KVL).*

The lake building boom—until the onset of the "Great Recession" (circa 2008)—brought with it more changes than many of the true locals cared to deal with, and for some, the final insult seems to have been the urban-style freeway system with its byzantine passages of bypasses, exit ramps and traffic arteries blasted through Osage Beach shortly into the first decade of the twenty-first century.

By 2012, one true local could no longer contain his views on the developments at the lake and mailed an edgy but well-reasoned and nuanced historical overview of the situation to the local weekly. The letter—for what it is and the information and emotion it conveys—would be difficult to improve upon. This quote is edited to exclude discussions of the Missouri Department of Transportation public hearings on the route and ramps of the new expressway and of the affairs of local businesses and persons:

> *In the past months I have had to read, weekly, a letter written by some angry, misguided soul who believes that businesses have been ruined due to our new bypass.*
>
> *First off, as a 40-year-old, third generation local whose families, on both sides saw their Mom and Pop resorts basically put out of business by the 80s condo rush, I speak from a level of experience in this matter.*
>
> *...Back when the condos came to town in my youth it was the beginning of the end for the Mom and Pop resorts that had dominated the lake for 30 years.*
>
> *It was called progress, and it was. See when we sold almost all of our shoreline to create "summer shacks" and the family owned resorts began to disappear, the condo's* [sic] *that replaced them hired a lot more people than the former, smaller resorts. So...most of the lake was actually better off...*
>
> *I'll venture that condos destroyed more family businesses than anything else here at the lake. Oh, but that was real progress, right?*
>
> *And while it decimated businesses that had been family run for generations, overall more lake residents prospered than were injured...*
>
> *Now times are tough and y'all want to point fingers and such. Ironically, the people, like my family, true locals that remember the eight months of barren roads every year never point fingers at others.*
>
> *We, the folks whose great-great grandparents lived here before the lake was green, back when Carl Williams and Lee Mace owned most of Osage Beach, back when my dad...flew kites and jumped ramps for the 60s era ski show.*[1]

The condominium model made a great deal of sense for developers at the Lake of the Ozarks. A two-hundred-foot shoreline would under the "old lake" formula be divided into four fifty-foot lots and end up with four small weekend cabins or summer houses on it. But if the formula is revised to include vertical space, the resulting product can be dramatically enhanced. Instead of four fifty-foot lots, there can be an eight-story building with multiple units per floor. That fact in itself is weighty enough to have encouraged Lake of the Ozarks developers to go condo, but there is more to the story.

Monte Davidson entered this narrative as a central character in the chapter on the establishment of the lake's luxury resorts and the musical entertainment scene in the 1960s, but he still had more to contribute to this story.

As to why Osage Beach did not become the "Live Entertainment Capital of the World" (a sometime Branson marketing tag)—Monte D. (among others) said the reason is simple: "The business community didn't want it. They wanted to build condominiums."[2]

The primary marketing profile sought by Osage Beach was not the tour buses and early bird diners that throng to the "Shepherd of the Hills Country" town. (In other words, transient tourism was considered a secondary market and had not been on the radar of the Lake of the Ozarks commercial culture for a long time.) Rather, Osage Beach aimed to attract the urban refugees who wanted to live year round (or at least full season) in lakeside condos and sup at gourmet or upscale restaurants, shop at malls, play golf four times a week if not more often, patronize movie theaters where frozen margaritas were available at the snack bar and lounge poolside or cruise on their yachts out on the lake the rest of the time—the affluent, constant consumers.

There could have been country music shows, but they would have been of the nature exemplified by Monte D. and Lee Mace—that is, with appeal to both "mountain folk" (people from the region) and city "sophisticates" (the condo-dwelling transplants).

There is no question that Lee Mace, one of the earliest of the region's champions, clearly understood the commercial direction of the lake. In the late 1970s, he had remarked that in the future, competition for audiences would not be other shows but the restaurants.[3]

There are indications that Mace planned to create a Grand Ole Opry–style operation built on the success of his Ozark Opry, but he would not live to fully implement those plans.

With the death of Lee Mace in 1985, the possibility of a major music industry at Osage Beach faded, and the remaining vision was to attract urban retirees or refugees to live at the Lake of the Ozarks—the more the better.

It is a simple matter to view the future through the lens of the local business community of the 1980s, which envisioned a cosmopolitan aura to the soon-to-be sophisticated Osage Beach (St. Louis) side of the lake. This aura may attract corporate headquarters and their highly paid corporate jet-setting executives. A stable, wealthy permanent population could make it all happen.[4]

CONCLUSION

(KVL)

Our story tapers off at about the turn of the century. Although there is some notice of twenty-first century doings herein, the issues of the lake were, at the time of this writing, fluid and dynamic, calling for interpretation by journalists rather than historians. In conclusion, we offer this summary and a look, to the extent possible, into the future with Internet references of post-text events.

The four rural Missouri counties of Benton, Camden, Miller and Morgan, located in the south central part of the state, were typical rural America counties, characterized by sparse population and an agrarian, "live off the land" lifestyle. The members of this community were generally white and Protestant. They interacted in small groups and lived in an almost cashless society. Much of the economic survival was based on bartering. The necessary staples represented the majority of cash-purchased items.

This lifestyle existed generally unchanged from the time the "white" population began to migrate into the area during the late 1700s into the early twentieth century. The late 1920s brought a change in living characteristics to these counties not seen in America in the prior period.

The following decade saw America in the depths of the Great Depression, with high unemployment and people living in despair. The four counties that we call the "Lake of the Ozarks area" or simply the "lake area" did not experience this economic devastation. Many residents stated "there was no Depression here." There were major changes taking place, and the region would take on characteristics not before seen in rural America this time.

Unbeknownst to the residents and many others, over a time period of less than eighty years, much of the area would be functioning like a city. It had become urbanized, taking on the traits of a city, unlike anything seen before, right in very rural central Missouri.

Our mission has been to take a look at this region and identify the causation factors behind this phenomenal change to this rural area. It is a remarkable story, and there are few similar tales of domestic cultural shock on such scale.

The beginning of this change, or crystallization factor, was the vision of a few people who saw the Osage River as a profitable place to build a hydroelectric power plant. This visualization became a reality, with construction beginning in 1929 and completed in 1931.

The Osage Project supported an area-wide economic boom not seen in other parts of the state and country at that time. It was reported there were as many as four thousand people employed in the specific dam construction process. Many had access to living arrangements within the construction camp, which included houses and dormitories, a mess hall, a hospital, a commissary and a school.

Those who were not employed in the actual dam construction found other employment in related jobs, such as clearing land below the water line area of trees, tearing down and moving buildings and relocating cemeteries.

There were related support jobs also—which, in hindsight, may have been the catalyst to bigger activities that led to complete and irreversible cultural change. People who came to the area—workers and non-workers alike—wanted places to eat, maybe a place to stay, some type of entertainment and to tour and see the dam. Naysayers said the dam would never hold water, and many said it wouldn't fill up in their lifetimes.

Through the 1930s Depression era and early 1940s World War II era, the lake area did raise some interest as a hunting and fishing venue, and people also started to show interest in on-the-water activities. This was a time when people did not have much expendable cash for leisure activities.

The post–World War II and early 1950s era was a period when people had many employment opportunities. Along with jobs, people began to have benefits, including vacations, and better roads were being built for travel. The lake area capitalized on these economic changes, identified by visionaries, area leaders and focused businesses.

The area became known as a destination. People would come to visit and stay at travel courts and small resort cabins. They would participate in area sightseeing, outdoor activities and just enjoy the area.

From the 1960s through the 1980s, the area really solidified its move into a full-fledged urban region. It clearly began presenting the basic characteristics of urbanization, including a variety of employment opportunities and urban-style business, such as hospitals, supermarkets and retail businesses. Permanent housing facilities were also being built.

The pains of becoming an urban area also became pronounced in this time period. Being a rural multicounty area, an over-reaching governmental unit did not exist. Couple this lack of regulation with the phenomenon of increased numbers of people living or visiting the area and the result was a severe strain on managing the land and resources.

The existence of small incorporated areas coupled with large unincorporated areas within geographically large counties, all of which surround a large investor-owned lake with free public access, led to a "who is responsible" situation. This produced challenges in addressing urban-style issues, such as the public service issues of waste and potable water, public safety, building codes, identification of responsible parties and general planning for the growing area.

The lack of overall responsibility of these urban-style issues led to multiple challenges. Items of growth will need to be addressed. The future of this area will be shaped by the methods used to address challenges. In the future, development questions will arise and be addressed. These issues may be addressed by taking a "no action" stance, therefore the issue is addressed via a default of no action.

The now urban area will change. The change will be directed by visionaries who will take the lead for the area's future or a unified, overseeing body. This body must also implement and enforce standards for environmental issues of potable water, sewage and solid waste.

It is a known fact that things change. The lake area will change as people change and the world changes. The challenge for the area will be *how* it changes. Well-known vacation and resort areas have suffered identifiable decline. A couple notable areas are the Poconos and the Catskills. Since the lake area has grown to be more than a resort area and now functions as a city, there is reason to believe it will continue to exist as an urban area.

Its existence as an urban area will depend on leadership and chosen direction. One just has to look at America's past cities in the Rust Belt, the automotive giant Detroit or the nonexistent mining towns across the country. Did each have an answer for repurposing itself?[1]

The real story for the lake area is how it is going to address change. An often noted belief states, "It is not the strongest that survive, nor is it the most intelligent. It is those who adapt to change." The future of the Lake of the Ozarks will be determined by how it adapts to change. The theory of social change is very dynamic—another story for another time.

APPENDIX A

A PEOPLE'S PROSPECTUS

As noted in the introduction, our definition of "A People's History" is a work that not only recounts events, persons, ideas and ideals associated with specified times and the spirit of those times (*zeitgeist*) but also explores how these things were generally encountered and interpreted as human experience.

All histories require the perspective of things past—it is impossible to write a history of current events. As noted in the conclusion of this book, the present tense is the domain of the journalist. For additional clarity on the subject, we are indebted to Eric Larsen for his quote from Marilynne Robinson about the divide between the language of history and that of contemporary events: "The language of present experience is so charged with judgement and illusion and intonation that it cannot be put to any new use or forced along any unaccustomed path."

What we can know of present experience (that of the indeterminate immediate) is, however, ceded from the past. We can see that much of the animus that historically hovered between the lake's true locals and those who later settled is greatly a product of cultural determinism—the sense that a particular way of life is correct and other ways are less correct. We also know of cultural assimilation, which is one way "home" is discovered or created. This latter positive process is obvious all across the Lake of the Ozarks region. Those who were latecomers are becoming "Lakers" or even (in the future) true locals—perhaps slowly but nevertheless so.

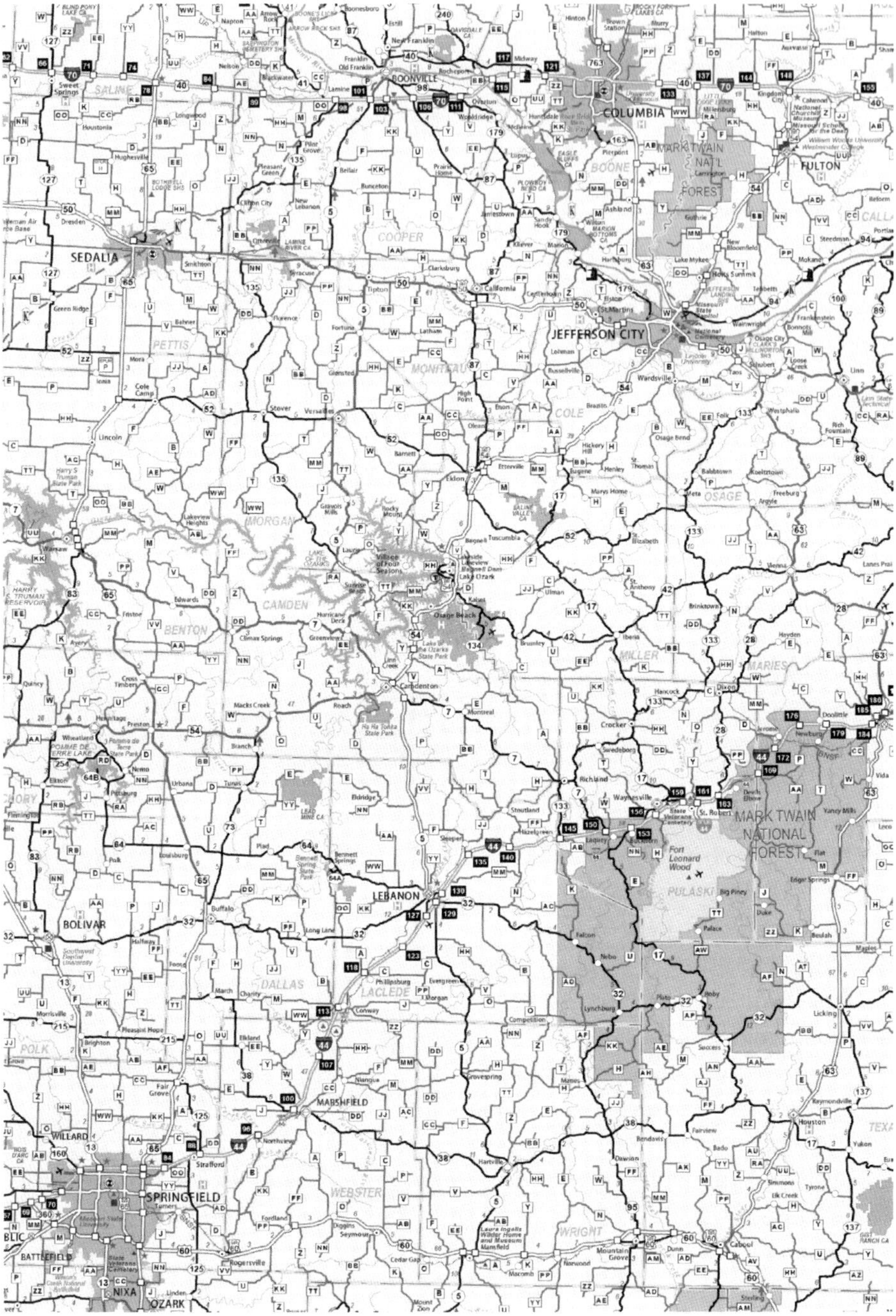

This map of the four-county area in central Missouri displays the focal point and location of the Lake of the Ozarks. *Courtesy of the Missouri Department of Transportation.*

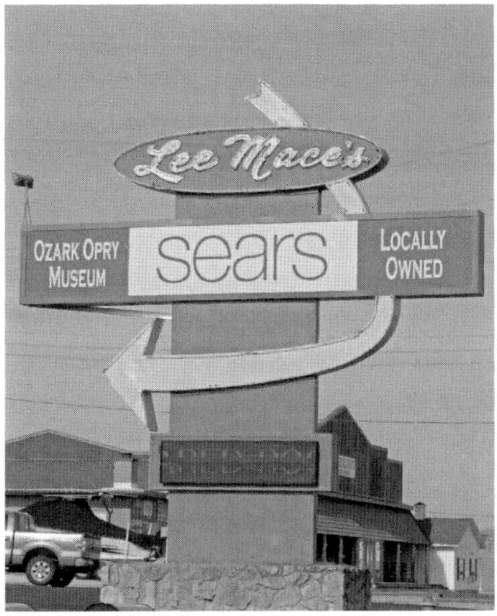

This sign was originally used for the famous Lee Mace's Ozark Opry Theater. The theater building has become a Sears catalogue store. It is an example of repurposing the famous sign and building without moving either one. *Author's personal collection (KVL).*

We concluded the writing of this book during the second decade of the twenty-first century, scant years into the centennial of the creation of the Lake of the Ozarks. During these decades, the lake-area population had begun to move toward establishing an infrastructure that seemed to signify a *positive* acceptance of the lake's urban nature and the need for reinvention based on that acceptance.

This urbanization process was perhaps most visible in the "repurposing" of properties and structures, as in the twenty-first-century reincarnation of Lee Mace's Ozark Opry building as a retail store or the conversion of some of the older "tourist camp"–style motels into apartment housing.

A significant sign of this cultural movement was the construction of the Community Bridge in the late 1990s. The span connected the west side (from Sunrise Beach) to the east side (Osage Beach) for the first time in the over seventy-year history of the Lake of the Ozarks. What had been a fairly daunting drive around the lakeshore to get to the other side of the lake became a matter of minutes on the new toll bridge.

Further civic awakening—coming after over seven decades of neglect and negligence—seemed to have been sparked by the action of the Federal Energy Regulatory Commission (FERC) requirements for Ameren's renewal of the Bagnell Dam (Osage Project) relicensing.

The license period is for forty years—there had been a previous license renewal, but it gave all appearance of being "rubber stamped." Not so as the century turned. Ameren UE (the successor to Union Electric and predecessor of Ameren Missouri) was required to develop and submit a "Shoreline Management Plan" for FERC approval—which was done, as was the 2003 establishment of a Shoreline Management Office on the Willmore Lodge property.

The licensing renewal was eventually approved after a few years of wrangling with the public and media about the actual boundaries of the lake (it was estimated several thousand private first-tier structures encroached on the "Project," and until FERC agreed to allow Ameren to negotiate with the owners of lakeside land that were affected, the licensing process was disrupted).

In the early days of the lake—when housing and boating structures were most often of an improvised nature or, better stated, of vernacular construction—it was customary to float docks on empty fifty-five-gallon drums salvaged from one industrial source or another. As the drums rusted out, the remnants of whatever they had previously contained was released into the lake—not a desirable development, but there was little general concern, and there were no government regulations of private docks at that time.

Then from latter twentieth century to the first decade of the twenty-first century, most docks were kept afloat with large, fully exposed polystyrene blocks (commonly referred to as "foam"), which eroded with constant exposure to water and wind, releasing clouds of tiny pellets that coated the surface of much of the lake. This sea of polystyrene was increased as a considerable number of the mother blocks broke free from dock fastenings due to boat wakes and rough weather. This unnatural and ugly skein made for an unpleasant visual of the lake waters.

As the Bagnell Dam (Osage Project) relicensing requirement deadline with FERC approached and was initially addressed by Ameren (roughly 2003–07), the utility company issued an order for all dock floatation supports on the lake to be encapsulated. This encapsulation order—which had no "grandfather" provision but allowed a reasonable time for implementation—had an astonishing effect on the lake. By the second decade of the century, the lake was perhaps near as clear and litter free as it had been since its inception.

To be direct and straightforward: FERC in the twenty-first century was the first government entity to have—and assert—regulatory jurisdiction over the entire lake region since the dam had been constructed. And it appears the general effect was immediate.

There was a rippling effect, perhaps best symbolized by the story of the Rocky Mount Sewer District founding. One of the challenges for many residents of the lake was the lack of central sewage service—again, a result of unplanned urbanization. The privately owned lake shoreline was intensely developed but historically had little concern with the disposal of waste.

For decades, this matter of concern was more or less ignored. But as the twenty-first century progressed, local governments and community and citizen organizations turned their attentions and efforts to the problem of sewage disposal.

That the effort was determined and hard fought is evident in the following excerpted letter to the editor from the December 18, 2014 *Versailles Leader-Statesman* from Judy Kenworthy, treasurer of the Rocky Mount Sewer District Board (RMSDB). Kenworthy seemed to work from a list of the most common opposition arguments, dismissing each in turn. First there was the matter of "treated effluent…destroying the habitat of the Niangua darter fish." Not possible, Kenworthy noted, because "that little fish cannot be found in the Lake of the Ozarks."

She then derided the argument that the lake's famous population of American eagles might not want to nest near treated effluent—certainly, she argued, those noble birds would prefer such effluent to raw sewage.

Residents of a certain subdivision were unhappy that treated effluent would flow into "their" cove. Kenworthy responded: "The cost of protecting the Lake must be borne by the current owners; the benefit will fall to family and friends who enjoy the Lake long after we are gone."

After a further reading of the Riot Act, Kenworthy pulled the trigger: "The Sewer Board will continue our efforts to preserve the Lake for future generations. We will not give up until we have accomplished our goal."

And Kenworthy and her board members succeeded. The August 20, 2015 issue of the *Leader-Statesman* ran a full-page article headlined "Rocky Mount Sewer System Plant in Ground," which included a vow from an RMSBD official to eventually provide a "central sewer district to all 1,900 homes in the District."

Our judgement is that for most of this coming century, the impulses and actions of the lake region population will be toward achieving and maintaining an attractive and viable habitat. This judgement arises in great part from the emergence in the early twenty-first century of dedicated citizens' organizations, such as the Lake Ozark Watershed Alliance (LOWA); the determination of groups like the RMSDB; the regulatory authority asserted by the Federal Energy Regulatory Commission (FERC); and the demonstrations of good corporate citizenship by Ameren Missouri, among other positive forces operating to improve and maintain healthy ecological and civic conditions at the lake.

Our further speculation is that the urbanization of the lake region will stabilize its future as a tourist, retirement and recreational destination. The continuing diversification of population and occupation will create a solid foundation for growth and prosperity, supporting wage-earning, professional and entrepreneurial classes.

We should also note that the urban region at the turn of the twenty-first century was defined by a one- to ten-mile distance from the lakeshore. The urban pattern webbed out from the Osage Beach and Community Bridge area and lessened with distance. The farther the actual distance from the lake's shoreline, the less influence there exists to fully embody all the characteristics of an urban area. For example, both Eldon and Osage Beach identify themselves with the lake—Eldon is "The Gateway to the Lake of the Ozarks " (as is Gravois Mills on the lake's Kansas City side), and Osage Beach proclaims itself somewhat grandly to be *the* "Lake of the Ozarks." However, a short drive to the northernmost population of the Tri-County area reveals that Morgan County's Versailles declares itself to be simply where the "Prairies Meet the Hills." The impression is that of a "central" city (Osage Beach and parts of Miller County), a "near" suburban area and a far suburban area.

A quick review of the definition of an "urbanized area": "contains a central populated place and all the surrounding 'closely settled' incorporated or unincorporated areas…the central populated place can be located a long way from the area that is urbanizing."

"Closely settled" may be defined as an area in which the "average building spacing is less than 100 feet."

This description fits the majority of the developed first-tier Lake of the Ozarks shoreline and the urbanized district around the properties that were once owned by the Willmore and Koplar interests.

The following briefs will be of interest to those who seek further insight into the future of the Lake of the Ozarks.

(1) One of the first signs of the positive effect of government regulation (FERC) was the Ameren order to encapsulate foam, discussed earlier. An Ameren media release on the subject can be found at http://ameren.mediaroom.com/index. php?s=43&item=570.

(2) A persisting concern in the early twenty-first century was that much of the electrical service to private docks was provided by unqualified installers. Local governments and Ameren had begun programs to correct this issue, but decades of the "no codes no planning no zoning" tradition in Missouri (See 2002 Brookings Report) had created thousands of structures with faulty wiring that more than often enough resulted in tragedy. More information can be found at http://lakeexpo.com/news/lake_news/

swimmer-electrocuted-at-lake-of-the-ozarks/article_25de24fe-1929-11e5-8ca0-0ff78a16476d. html.

(3) As noted previously, most small lot development at the lake did not account for sewage disposal. This issue, however, was being vigorously addressed by the dawn of the twenty-first century, and further information can be found at http://lakeexpo.com/news/lake_news/water-quality-issues-at-lake-of-the-ozarks-have-been/article_0c3e7644-a57a-11e3-ac36-001a4bcf887a.html.

(4) The Ameren Shoreline Management Plan (SMP) included a review of "Project Boundaries. "At the time of this writing, the controversy continued. The Ameren SMP can be viewed at http://lakeexpo.com/news/lake_news/ameren-to-diligently-enforce-new-shoreline-regulations/article_9b2fcc3a-8ad8-11e2-aa64-001a4bcf887a.html.

(5) A discussion of the 1980 Hancock Amendment to the Missouri Constitution does not fall within our definition of a "People's" history in that its detrimental socioeconomic effects, while culturally based, were politically sustained and culturally self-inflicted. However, we would be remiss in not encouraging further study.

The Hancock Amendment to the Missouri Constitution was voted in by the populace in 1980. The core of the law was the annual Missouri tax revenue could not exceed 5.6395 percent of the total personal income of the state's residents. Court challenges and revisions followed immediately, and the amendment was altered dramatically by judicial and legislative actions. Still, as a 2011 news report noted, "The spirit of Hancock's goal to limit Missouri revenue has lived on."

As one commentator, referring to the Hancock Amendment, explained: "It shifted state responsibility to the local level for many social and community needs, created more earmarked taxes and took flexibility away from the state legislature and helped spur the use of tax credits."

Noted also was the fiscally crippling Hancock consequence of a heavy reliance on sales tax income to fund services in Missouri civic entities.

The tale of the "Mack's Creek Law" is a must read. Further information can be found at http://www.stltoday.com/news/local/govt-and-politics/changes-to-missouri-tax-credit-programs-face-continued-obstacles/article_8d5c1b84-5ff6-52ba-b5f4-f50883580bd3.html; https://mospace.umsystem.edu/xmlui/bitstream/handle/10355/2888/HancockAmendmentMissourisTax.pdf?sequence=1; and https://en.wikipedia.org/wiki/Macks_Creek,_Missouri.

Appendix B

RESORTS FOR BLACKS AT THE LAKE OF THE OZARKS[1]

(KVL)

As tourist business development started as early as the 1950s, the lake area was focused on the white population. Critical population data will show that the area white population was over 95 percent. The majority of the lake-area black population was in the Versailles area. As we developed our writings, we wanted to see if any black-focused business activity existed. We identified three documented resorts that served mainly black customers. They were Lake Placid in western Morgan County, Duncan's Point Resort on the Lake and McField's Oakridge Resort in the Osage Beach area.

Lake Placid has a very unique history. The lake was developed by Dr. Percy C. Turner out of Kansas City."Lake Placid: 'A Recreational Center for Colored People in the Missouri Ozarks,'" a chapter in *Race and Menaning*, by Gary R. Kremer and Evan P. Orr, introduces Dr. Turner and his partner, J.M. Sojourner: "On October 8, 1934, during the heart of the Great Depression and in the second year of Franklin Delano Roosevelt's first term as president of the United States, two white men from Morgan County, Missouri, sold a 346-acre plot of land in the Missouri Ozarks to two black men from Kansas City. The sellers were a prominent county physician, and his son-in-law, a local farmer named Reed Blackman."

The article goes on to note the buyers were the superintendent of General Hospital No. 2 in Kansas City (Turner) and a printer and owner of the Sojourner Press, also of Kansas City. The two men were seeking to establish a lake getaway where blacks could relax while escaping the relentless racial segregation of the times.

Turner and Sojourner followed a pattern of development of the property that would match that of the later Willmore et al platting of the Lake of the Ozarks shoreline: "Individual lots measuring 33 1/3 x 100 feet would be sold at prices ranging from fifty dollars to one hundred dollars, depending on the location." Ninety-six acres of the property was to be reserved for a lake, a dam and a golf course.

Turner, the lead partner, was truly a visionary and a determined one at that—there seems little question that he was inspired by the future of the then nascent Lake of the Ozarks. The property purchased, in Morgan County, was comprised of steep, rocky upland—typical Ozarks mountain terrain—of little practical use. There was no dam, lake or golf course and even imagining such amenities that far back in the hills would have required considerable daydreaming.

And to expect an African American partnership could negotiate to purchase land in the 1930s interior Ozarks at reasonable terms—or at all—also would have somewhat strained credibility. It is likely the times worked in their favor; this was the fifth year of the Great Depression, and cash money and buyers for Ozarks real estate were in short supply.

So the partners made a "creative financing" offer that called for the sellers holding the debt, $2 down and the balance to be paid as a percentage of proceeds from the sales of lots—until a total of $22,000 had been paid, thereby retiring the mortgage. Reed Blackman and his father-in-law accepted.

"Thus, Turner and Sojourner agreed to pay the considerable sum of more than $63.58 per acre for rocky, hilly, tree covered northern Ozarks land. This represented at least three times the per acre cost of similar land in the area. The advantage to Turner and Sojourner, of course, was that they could pay off their indebtedness to the sellers from the proceeds earned from selling lots."

What happened next is possibly of most interest—Turner applied to the federal government for assistance to build a dam on the property thereby to create the lake (platted as a "reservoir") that would be the centerpiece of Lake Placid.

On May 6, 1935, FDR issued Executive Order 7034 creating the Works Progress Administration (WPA), which was renamed Works Projects Administration in 1939. The initial appropriation for the program was $5 billion. The money was to be spent for the public good, funding anything and everything from projects in the arts and letters to construction of bridges and ditches. One of the funded projects was Lake Placid.

Duncan's Point Resort on the lake was developed by Kansas City businessman Daniel R. Duncan. In 1953, Duncan started with a 71-acre purchase from owner the Willmore Lake Company and, six months later, purchased an additional 168 acres.

Duncan overcame racial discrimination and physical barriers to develop a viable resort community. The resort was known as a haven for residents and guests as a peaceful and relaxing alternative to hectic city life.

Duncan's Point heritage was recognized by the Missouri Department of Natural Resources and is eligible for inclusion in the National Register of Historic Places

McField's Oakridge Resort, in the Osage Beach area, was developed by Limuel McField. While he was a student at Lincoln University in Jefferson City, he would come to the lake area for work. This started his dream of developing a location that would welcome blacks. He purchased a thirteen-acre tract with some existing cottages and started renting to Jefferson City people in 1939. During Oakridge Resort's early years, McField found it difficult to obtain financial loans from lending institutions. He and his family did much of the renovation work on the existing cottages.

Oakridge Resort saw major facilities and financial changes in the 1950s and 1960s. In the 1960s, local banks became very willing to give McField financial support for additional permanent construction projects.

Additional and notable recognition must be made of Limuel and Beatrice McField's success in the community. Limuel was appointed by the City of Osage Beach to oversee and serve on the wastewater treatment and sewer boards and to chair the Planning and Zoning Commission and the Industrial Development Corporation. His wife was the first nursing supervisor at the new Lake of the Ozark Hospital and was involved in community clubs.

One could surmise the McFields were among the first black residents to hold notable positions in the predominantly white lake area, a big step for the rural Missouri Ozarks.

Appendix C

SPOONBILLS (AND STRIPERS)[1]

The central themes of this narrative have arisen from the cultural and social impact of the creation of the Lake of the Ozarks on the human population of the region. However, failure to note the impacts on wildlife in the area would be remiss. The fate of the paddlefish yields a most useful story.

Toward the late 1900s, some of the effects of the nineteenth- and early twentieth-century liquidation cutting of the Ozarks forests and the slaughter to extirpation of any and all edible or usable animal life were showing signs of reversal. Elk had been reintroduced to the southern Missouri Ozarks, and wild turkey and deer populations had attained sufficient supply statewide to sustain lengthy hunting seasons and to lure predator species back to the region. Cougar had been spotted in various Missouri locales and even caught on video, while black bear (*Ursus Americanus*) could be considered greatly restored in some of their Ozarks habitat.

To the extent possible, the Ozarks forest had more or less returned, mostly with second and third growth but nonetheless there.

It should be noted that, one way or another, what had occurred in the lengthy "clear cutting" era of the Ozarks was that much of the "natural resources"—the forests, the game animals and, for that matter, the minerals—had been converted to personal wealth, use or corporate enrichment.

It is important to note that there was no significant federal environmental protection legislation or regulation prior to the Pittman-Robertson Act of 1937, and the Environmental Protection Agency was not created until

1970. Five years before the Robertson Act, in April 1932, as the Lake of the Ozarks was swelling toward spillway crest elevation, a citizen's solution to the stocking of the new lake was implemented. T.T. McKinnon, the superintendent of Kansas City's Swope Park Zoo, traveled to the region to supervise—with the assistance of Game Warden W.W. Smoyer and a number of local volunteers—the stocking of the waters behind the dam. The method was simple: seine-haul fishing of Ozarks streams for supplies of native game fish, which were then transported to and dumped into the new lake.

Problem solved—Lake of the Ozarks fish were stocked until 1979, when a serious problem with such arose, as was recounted in an August 23, 2004 letter from Troutman Sanders LLP—Ameren's attorney—to the United States Fish and Wildlife Service:

> *Paddlefish do not reproduce naturally at the Project because their spawning grounds were flooded by an Army Corps of Engineers Project known as the Harry S. Truman Dam ("HST Dam") which is upstream from Ameren UE's Project. In fact, paddlefish exist at the project only as a result of a put, take and grow fishery supported by a hatchery financed by Ameren UE under its FERC license.*

Ozarkers are, as a culture, fond of their paddlefish (*Polyodon spathula*), often called "spoonbills" by the locals—a reference to the lengthy spatula-like rostrum the species sports. Paddlefish have the estimated ability to live twenty to fifty years and to grow up to five feet (measured from eye to fork of tail).

Paddlefish are said to have been around in the age of dinosaurs and, like their distant relative the shark, have skeletons consisting largely of cartilage. The species feed by swimming with their mouth open, filtering for the plankton that is their diet. For this reason, the only way to catch a spoonbill is to "snag" it. Despite the term, Missouri Department of Conservation (MDC) asks that fishers use nets rather than gaffes to avoid fatally injuring sublegal paddlefish. It is unknowable as to what extent the request is honored, but it is not illegal to gaff the fish.

In addition to legal snagging—the paddlefish season in Missouri generally in the twentieth century ran from March 15 through April 30—conservation agents and other law enforcement had to halt illegal trafficking in paddlefish caviar. No one can say how big this black market was, but in 2012, it was reported the MDC had broken up an "international" paddlefish poaching operation in the Warsaw, Missouri area that was characterized as "large scale."

The paddlefish present a couple problems in their physical characteristics and spawning habits for those who would attempt to assure their continued survival in the Lake of the Ozarks region. Paddlefish sense their world through electromagnetic organs that are apparently quite sensitive—so much so that the fish cannot pass through concrete fish ladders because the rebar used in concrete construction disrupts their sensory systems.

The spoonbill's spawning is also a problem. They have to lay their eggs in flowing shallows on sandbars or exposed gravel, to which the eggs adhere while incubating. That habitat having been removed, it was up to the "put, take and grow" method of keeping the species alive.

The MDC youth publication *Xplor* published an interview—excerpted below—with hatchery manager Bruce Drecktrah under its "Wild Jobs" banner on March 28, 2013:

> *Q: How do you gather their (Paddlefish) eggs?*
>
> *A: When females are ready to lay, we lift them out of the water and catch the eggs in a pan. Paddlefish are heavy, so another hatchery worker helps me lift them. Luckily, paddlefish have a built-in handle.*
>
> *Q: What do you do with the eggs?*
>
> *A: We add a few more ingredients and stir the mixture with a turkey feather. Paddlefish eggs are delicate. If we stirred with anything else, we'd scramble the eggs.*
>
> *Q: How long does it take the eggs to hatch?*
>
> *A: About a week. The baby paddlefish live in an aquarium for a few days, then we move them outside to ponds. When they're big enough to fend for themselves, we turn them loose in Truman Lake, Table Rock Lake and the Lake of the Ozarks.*
>
> *Q: Why not let the paddlefish lay eggs in the wild?*
>
> *A: Dam building and river dredging has destroyed many places where paddlefish lay eggs. Without hatcheries, paddlefish would disappear from many of Missouri's waters.*

Note the requirement of stirring the fish eggs with a turkey feather—probably not a function that can be mechanized.

As part of the licensing agreement for the dam—issued by the Federal Energy Regulatory Commission (FERC)—Ameren Missouri paid for a portion of the hatchery service.

In this sense, the lake and dam are the ultimate clear cut. The fish affected must be reintroduced to their native—but now altered—habitat each year, or they will die out in the region. The MDC refers to each year's crop as a class and has noted that the average life of most of each class is less than ten years.

NOTES

Introduction

1. The oldest documented lilac bushes in the United States, planted in 1750, grace the Wentworth Coolidge Estate in Portsmouth, New Hampshire. There are undocumented assertions that date to 1630 the lilacs at the William Brewster home at the Pilgrims' Plymouth Plantation in Massachusetts.
2. For more information, search the phrase "TnGenes—Peek, Robert" at http://www.tngenes.net/index.php/mmilitary/civil-war/confederates/793-peek-robert-25th-tennessee-infantry/.
3. For more information, search the phrases "Calloway Manes" and "Mabel Manes Mottaz" at http://www.oldstagecoachstop. org/webgeezer/Gazette12/pages%2041%20Calloway%20Manes.pdf.
4. Dohm, "Political Culture of Missouri."

Chapter 1

1. Although it is possible Cravens had plans including development of lakeshore property, there appears to have been no visioning beyond accomplishment of the dam construction.
2. Gist and Fava, *Urban Society*. (KVL) The influential urban social anthropologist Noel Gist viewed the subject as a matter of practical function: "The accuracy of a definition of 'rural' and 'urban' is

not innate or fixed, but depends on the usefulness of the resulting categories. If businessmen, politicians, government, and researchers find rural-urban classifications do not help in analyzing or predicting community events, then the definition is not valid no matter how precise it may be."

(DWP) There existed in the 1920s a considerable material culture gap between "outstate" Missouri and the two major cities of the state. St. Louis had widened this leap when it updated its physical infrastructure in preparation for the 1904 World's Fair and was in that regard the equal of any of the great cities around the globe, "with its modern lights and purified water, skyscrapers and electric streetcar system" among other things, as Margot McMillen noted in *The Golden Lane*.

Chapter 2

1. See http://www.chrisanddavid.com/caddo (The Old Wire Road) and http://en.wikipedia.org/wiki/Old_Wire_Road. Sections of the Wire Road were known variously as the "Osage Trail," "Springfield Road," "Wilderness Road" and "Ridge Road" (Rafferty, *Ozarks*). The Missouri Department of Conservation (MDC) maintains conservation areas that include fragments of Native American traces in Dent County and Harrison County. The "Harmony Mission Trace" passed through what is now the Lake of the Ozarks region (Williams and Williams, "History of Versailles and Morgan County").
2. General Ivy, June 30, 1927 (courtesy Bill and Dorothy Williams and Morgan County Historical Society—transcription by Elaine Hardin). Otto Ernest Rayburn, writing in 1941, provided validation of General Ivy's recollection: "Pork has been the principal meat in the Ozarks since wild game became scarce" (Rayburn, *Ozark Country*). Gerard Schultz wrote that in the early nineteenth century, Ozarks "farm animals were bred and kept with a minimum of care" (Schultz, *Northern Ozarks*).
3. "Elk Return to Missouri," http://mdc.mo.gov/newsroom/elk-return-missouri-after-150-year-absence/.
4. Without steam, efficient transport on most Ozark waterways would have been impractical: "In spite of navigation problems and the danger of explosion, the steamboat was a great improvement over keelboats and flatboats, which had to be pulled, poled or paddled" (Rafferty, *Ozarks*).

5. *History of the Lake of the Ozarks*, video, October 14, 1987, moderated by Carl Williams with James Franklin Sr., M.R. "Doc" Foster, Albert Elam and Ernest McNeil, videographer Jim Phinney, courtesy Joyce Mace.

Chapter 3

1. Lest the impression be given that Ozarkers were the only clear-cutters, note that early settlers' deforestation of New England was such that by 1850, the forest cover of New Hampshire had been reduced to 45 percent from near 100 percent in pre-colonial times. See "Guide to New Hampshire Timber Harvesting Laws" at http://extension.unh.edu/resources/files/resource000253_rep274.pdf.
2. Sources reveal "log rolling" to have been an impressive enterprise: "The plaintiff in 1899 made a contract with the defendant by which he undertook to have made and delivered to the defendant one hundred thousand or more standard oak cross-ties...the company agreed to pay Goodrich 24 cents for each first-class tie and 9 cents for each cull tie, and one cent for loading each tie into cars for shipment" (*Bagnell Tie & Timber Co. v. Goodrich*).

Chapter 4

1. (KVL) The story of the Walton boys is well documented. Brothers Sam and James "Bud" Walton were in the small-town retail business by the middle of the twentieth century in the rural Ozarks of Missouri and Arkansas. These retail stores grew into what is known worldwide as the Walmart Corporation.

   Stated elsewhere in the text are the references to the work style and the agrarian and varied lifestyle of the Ozark native. They were hard workers—physical workers—with family values and capable of doing many jobs. It was well after World War II that wives and other females began working outside the home and almost never at a full-time job—they had their contributions/responsibilities at home.

   The Walton "discount" business model was developed with the idea to provide a certain number of common household items to the general public for a reasonable price and at a location near their homes. This allowed the Waltons' patrons to get their basic items fairly easily without wasting valuable time—an important factor in the agrarian/rural Ozark culture.

The labor for the early Walmart stores was provided by the local community. As the stores needed workers and the eligible workforce was small in numbers since many potential workers had other responsibilities at home and on the farm, Walmart, by necessity, followed a model of employing more people for only a few days a week—later called part-time employment.

This worked well for Walmart and the locals. It even allowed for youth and high school students to get after-school jobs. In the beginning, many Walmart jobs were paying seventy-five cents to one dollar an hour, and people were pleased to get "cash money," especially in the small rural Ozark communities.

Walmart has grown into a worldwide corporation. The federal and state governments have established many employment regulations, and employment in the rural Ozarks has changed, as it has elsewhere throughout the rest of the country.

These changes are outside the realm of this book. Best remember that the "Walton boys"—both deceased—started their business in order to provide basic goods to the rural community. A part of this model was the employment of local residents, who worked on a part-time schedule that could be compatible with their home and farm responsibilities. See books by Vance Randolph and Milton Rafferty regarding Ozark natives' work habits.

Chapter 5

1. The official motive and reasoning for both the JSLB and the government-sponsored federal mortgage enterprises such as Fannie Mae (1938) and Freddie Mac (1970)—and other government-sponsored enterprise (GSE) entities such as the rural electric cooperatives—is that certain social benefits are too necessary for the public good to forgo but too risky or unprofitable for private enterprise to deliver and therefore require government backing. But, the reasoning continues, private enterprise must still be given a piece of the action. See Nocera, "Fannie"; Bennett, "Joint Stock."
2. Undated letter from Morrill to Longworth (date stamped February 8, 1930). On March 6, 1916, as the bill creating the JSLBs was being

considered—it would pass into law in July of that year—the *New York Times* quoted an article from the "Journal of the American Bankers Association" pointing out the folly of the act. See "Rural Credit Plan Called Favoritism," at http://query.nytimes.com/mem/archive-free/pdf?res=F10913F93B5B17738DDDAF0894DB405B868DF1D3.

3. *Cravens v. United States*, 62 F. 2d 261 (8 Cir. 1932); *Cravens et al. v. United States*, no. 9235 (Circuit Court of Appeals, Eighth Circuit, November 28, 1932, rehearing denied, January 5, 1933).

Chapter 6

1. For Woodrow Wilson's "Federal Trade Commission Act," go to https://en.wikipedia.org/wiki/Federal_Trade_Commission_Act.
2. H. Dwight Weaver has written that Cravens was "suspected of misapplying $1,000,000 of the (Kansas City Joint Stock Land) banks funds…(Ralph) Street, who up to this time had been spending all his time overseeing work at the dam site, set about trying to salvage the project…and finally worked out a deal with Dillon, Read & Company and Stone & Webster (for) a loan…of $250,000…within a short time Union Electric had purchased the Osage Project." (*History and Geography of the Lake of the Ozarks—Volume One.* H. Dwight Weaver: Ozark River Trails, Eldon. 2005)

Chapter 7

1. Another way land could be obtained was by "Presidential Patent." This was a land grant from the federal government to an individual and that individual's posterity or assigns.
2. Lynn Morrow noted, "Homestead costs included a government fee, registration, commission and a word cost. Lands close to railroads were much higher than the usually quoted $1.25 per acre. A man would have to save cash payments for his labor at fifty cents a day to meet the fourteen- or sixteen-dollar filing fees."
3. For the early twenty-first-century high court rule on condemnation for private purpose see *Kelo v. City of New London* 545 U.S. 469—2005), a decision that demands notice. As reported in April 2014 in a syndicated newspaper column by Chuck Shepherd ("News of the Weird"):

> *A controversial landmark U.S. Supreme Court decision in 2005 for the first time allowed a city to force unwilling owners to sell private property not for a school or police station or other traditional municipal necessity, but just because a developer promised to improve the neighborhood. Consequently longtime residents such as Susette Kelo were forced off their land because the City of New London, Conn., had hopes of a prosperous buildup anchored by a new facility from the drug maker Pfizer. The* Weekly Standard *magazine reported in February, that nine years down the road Pfizer has backed out, and the 90-acre area of New London in which Kelo and others were bulldozed off of is waist high in weeds—an even worse blight than that which New London sacrificed private property rights to prevent.*

4. For contemporary reports on the UE-Snyder contretemps, "States & Cities: Lake of the Ozarks," *Time* magazine, December 14, 1931; "National Affairs: Damaged Ozarks," *Time* magazine, February 15, 1932.

Chapter 8

1. For an overview of American surveying history, see http://en.wikipedia.org/wiki/Public_Land_Survey_System.
2. The subject series of earthquakes included "three greater than magnitude 7, in 1811 and 1812. The quakes were so strong that the Mississippi River reportedly flowed backward, and church bells rang as far away as New England" ("Technology Offers Clues"). For an interesting sidebar, search online for "New Madrid Relief Act of 1815."
3. In the 1987 video, Al Elam stated that Cravens "had a deal with a judge up in Kansas City," perhaps to expedite the land transfers with as little scrutiny as possible. The samples viewed for this book were indeed all certified by the Jackson County court, but no further investigation of the allegation was undertaken.

Chapter 9

1. (KVL) It is not unusual for visitors to the Ozarks to remark on the custom of using full names in everyday life—"Billie Bob Blank" and so forth, due to surnames being passed from generation to generation and across family lines. Nicknames serve the same purpose. The names of children

who died in infancy or childhood were often conferred upon the next live birthed child of the same gender, the hope being that finally a member with the family's preferred given name would survive into adulthood.

Chapter 10

1. The region encompassing Missouri, Arkansas and contiguous western territory was referred to as the "Southwest" during the nineteenth century and the early twentieth century. The *Star* documented that the crowd at the lake opening weekend were indeed from all these then-termed "southwestern" states.
2. The report told of considerable optimism about the new body of water from these visitors. However, the common opinion of the native Ozarkers—the true locals—of the time was that the dam would never hold or that there would be insufficient river water to attain the needed depth. In his classic 1974 monograph *Before the Dam Water*, T. Victor Jeffries described the local sentiments thusly: "It was hard to visualize the water rising to the 660 level on the hill. An opponent of the dam told me one day he would drink every drop of the water if it ever got that high. The water got that high and I don't believe he drank any."
3. This steep offering price—a dollar per waterfront foot—may have contributed to the lack of shoreline property development under UE. This was, after all, during some of the most difficult years of the Great Depression.

Chapter 11

1. The reputation of the Lake of the Ozarks as a "party" destination will probably continue to wax and wane for as long as the lake exists. The commercial and promotional debate is about whether it is a "couples" or "family" venue. For a time in the late twentieth and early twenty-first century, the "couples" (read "party") concept carried the day, with resorts and restaurants like the Horny Toad and Peckers prominent. This trend faded, and the former became H. Toads, while the latter went out of business, as did most others with suggestive names. The promotional debate aside, the area of the lake known as the "Party Cove"—extant since the 1960s and dubbed by the *New York Times* the oldest such on-water

"permanent" debauchery—is perhaps most famous and durable of the so-called couples lot. There is indeed a whiff of the Pistol Club about it, and many locals view it with the same distaste accorded that long-gone club. http://www.nytimes.com/2005/07/22/travel/escapes/party-cove-wild-in-the-ozarks.html?_r=0/.

2. See *Citizens United v. Federal Election Commission* (no. 08-205, January 21, 2010); also related ruling in *McCutcheon v. Federal Election Commission* (no. 12-536, April 2, 2014).

Chapter 12

1. This is not to say the North American Company—which owned UE—complied meekly with the SEC divestiture rule. The holding company took its case to the U.S. Supreme Court. The court's response in denial:

> *North American is a typical utility holding company. It is the pinnacle of a great pyramid of corporations. As of December 21, 1940, there were some 80 corporations in the system, with an aggregate capitalized value in excess of $2,300,000,000. Organized in New Jersey in 1890 and maintaining business headquarters in New York City, North American maintains direct or indirect interests in these companies through the medium of stock ownership…*
>
> *The various companies in the North American system perform a variety of functions from electric and gas service to railroad transportation, warehousing and amusement park operations. All told, they conduct business in seventeen states and the District of Columbia. Electric service alone is provided for more than 3,000,000 customers in an area of roughly 165,000 square miles." (North American Company V. Securities and Exchange Commission. 327 U.S. 686)*

2. Willmore is notable in the relationship he established with the local population. He is described as gregarious and likeable. Unlike other city-based invaders of the Ozarks, he seems to have had the ability to personally connect with the locals. This may have been attributable to his apparent desire to live as an Ozarker. While the lake was central to his ambitions, he also aspired to be an Ozark cattle rancher, at one time running two thousand head on his lake properties. Of note, too, was Willmore's practice of offering lakefront property to his employees

in lieu of cash money wages. Although few took him up on the offer, it may have been regarded as a signifier of personal generosity. "Congress Repeals the Public Utility Holding Act of 1935," http://www2. gtlaw. com/pub/alerts/2005/0802.asp.

Chapter 13

1. "The Bonus Army," http://www.historynet.com/the-bonus-army-war-in-washington.htm.
2. A special advertising section sponsored by the Carnegie Corporation and Bill & Melinda Gates Foundation in the October 30, 2012 edition of *Time* magazine described the effect of the GI Bill education provision thusly: "[1944] President Franklin D. Roosevelt signs the GI BILL to help World War II veterans further their education. The bill fuels the growth of the middle class by making colleges and universities more affordable to people from all socioeconomic backgrounds."
3. "World War Two Merchant Mariners Seek Recognition, Compensation," http://www.pressdemocrat. com/article/20131110/articles/131119981. The obituary of a former WASP, Majorie Ellfeldt Rees, in the *Kansas City Star* of October 14, 2011, titled "She Made Every Day Count," recounted the official attitude toward the WASP service:

> *But the day she earned her pilots license, she signed up for a new government program called Women Airforce Service Pilots, or WASPs.*
>
> *She worked 18 months as a test pilot (mostly on B-25s), flying to air bases during World War II, doing everything that male military pilots did—except combat missions.*
>
> *At war's end the WASP program and all records of its existence were closed for security reasons, according to the government. The women stepped back into more maternal roles, and history forgot them.*
>
> *That changed in 1977 when the "fly girls" received full veteran status. In 2010, the WASPs were awarded the Congressional Gold Medal. Though thrilled, Marjorie told her family it was bittersweet. So many of the WASPs had died.*

It is certain the wartime experience of women taking occupations that had been theretofore male specific—the WASPs and "Rosie the Riveter" images being most historically visible—led to the same kinds of work diversification in post–World War II American life, including significantly the rural population, as will be discussed in later chapters.

4. What may be overlooked in the story of the post–World War II veteran benefit programs is that, coupled with the Great Depression experience of government-administered public employments—the WPA and CCC for example—not to mention distributions of food stuffs, known as "Commodities" (Later: "Government Cheese"), Ozarker traditional mistrust of such government-administered payments could have begun to lessen. Not to say that Ozarkers' mistrust and resistance to such programs disappeared during the twentieth century—it did not. Even those qualified for government-administered assistance in those days often did not avail themselves. Sometimes this reticence was due to lack of information, with residents mistakenly believing these programs to be "welfare." As will be noted later, rural tradition—that of the farm and hunt—is rooted in the direct connection between work and livelihood. And often this misperception was reinforced by underlying cultural criticism. In the 1930s, for example, when Social Security was introduced, it was called the "old age pension" in the Ozarks.

   In the lake region, however, a specific government-administered program supported a post–World War II new way of life: seasonal employment for cash money pay and off-season income from collection of unemployment insurance. Performers in Lee Mace's Ozark Opry, for example, received a "lay-off" letter at the end of each summer season that they could if desired present to collect on their unemployment insurance. This pattern of work and income was to become common to the lake culture—it was, however, not a topic for polite conversation.

5. See "Weber Grill," http://www.weber.com/about/the-birth-of-american-grilling.

Chapter 14

1. (KVL) Sociologist James West made note of the difference in rural and urban work in his 1945 study *Plainville, U.S.A.*

> *In fact, the great distinctive characteristics of rural work, contrasted with urban work are these: (1) the great variety of rural tasks, (2) the individual control of speed with which they are performed; (3) the freedom of the workers mind from "racket" (noise), overseers, and the tedium of strict,*

enforced, unsociable cooperation with other workers. Rural group work is, of course, highly social, but most rural work is done alone, or with a child "follering" (looking on). The solitary worker's mind is free to roam, dream, and scheme. (4) The immediate, personally understood, and simple relationship between work and livelihood.

These characteristics of rural work apply particularly to farmers, but they also apply to small-town businessmen. It is perhaps significant that while many Plainvillers were heard to complain of distasteful individual tasks, of having to work "too hard," and of poor rewards for their work no adult was heard to express general distaste for his work.

2. (KVL) As we discuss the lifestyles of our Missouri Ozarks in the early twentieth century, you will note there is limited discussion of social stratification. An observation of the locals reveals a rather narrow difference among the natives.

The material resources display some differences. The "well-to-do" natives lived in houses with running water, electricity and maybe a telephone and motorized vehicle. The other natives most likely did not have these "nicetics," mostly because availability was limited (of electricity, for example) and they lived outside of town.

We must remember, as discussed elsewhere, that this area relied on more of a barter-trading lifestyle with minimal cash transactions. As a young child, I remember our family doctor stating several times, "I made a house call (doctors made mostly house calls because they had cars, and the natives didn't) to Jessie and Sarah Pugh's last night." He remarked that they gave him a dozen eggs and a jar of Sarah's best homemade pickles in appreciation of the doctor's visit. We note the locals always referred to the doctor's "visit"; it was important to them that the doctor came to their home, and the message of a "visit" was very meaningful to the locals. The doctor was pleased and openly accepted these items as payment for his services.

The Ozark natives had a very narrow social stratification. The residents with great opulence were few and far between. Even those with large landholdings were not necessarily better off, mainly because of the generally poor land and the additional cost of production off of the land.

Those in the area who were considered as having a lot were quite often outsiders who came to the area using wealth earned elsewhere.

Chapter 15

1. Although it may be thought the Mace surname is of Native American origin—and there is considerable Osage Indian in the bloodline—Lois Webb has traced the family forebears of that name to England.
2. John Quincy Wolf, "Folksingers and the Re-Creation of Folksong," *Western Folklore* 26, no. 2 (April 1967), cited in a private communication with Kathryn Cunningham (DWP). This tradition of "unchanged" may be an extension of the old Ozarks cultural imperative that each generation live life virtually the same as the previous generation. As previously noted, by the twenty-first century, the likelihood of fulfilling this cultural requirement had diminished considerably.

   Neil Morris lived in the northern Arkansas Ozarks and was the father of James C. Morris, who as "Jimmy Driftwood" converted traditional melodies and themes to what Vance Randolph—with unmistakable disapproval—declared were "jukebox" tunes. "The Battle of New Orleans" was one of Driftwood's most commercially successful efforts and was set to "The 8th of January," an old fiddle tune celebrating that battle.

Chapter 16

1. Rafferty had observed that the White River was the only Ozark waterway of sufficient size to accommodate large steamboats. Most other rivers in the Ozarks were confined by size to smaller steamer craft that pushed barges or those that used small manpowered boats to move cargo.
2. "Shepherd of the Hills," http://en.wikipedia.org/wiki/The_Shepherd_of_the_Hills.

Chapter 18

1. *L.O. Profile* magazine, July–August 2010, Studio M Publishing LLC, Lake Ozark, Missouri.
2. (KVL) In the haste to construct the airport in time for the NGA conference, a section of the Lake of the Ozarks State Park was expropriated. This location, far from any conveniences and with obscure access to main highways, probably is a principal reason the anticipated interest from the airline industry never materialized. (The park encompasses a maze of

17,500 acres in Miller and Camden Counties and resembles a conservation area from the Teddy Roosevelt times). The following is from a July 20, 1969 report of the airport's genesis in the Jefferson City *News Tribune*:

> *The landing strip* [at the Lee C. Fine Memorial Airport at the Lake of the Ozarks] *will be 6,500 feet long and 100 feet wide. The strip, taxi area and tie-down locations will contain 104,000 cubic yards of concrete. The five-room terminal building at the Lee C. Fine Airport… reflects the rustic surroundings in which it nestles. The exterior is cedar, stained a rich brown. The roof is western cedar shake shingles. The building measures approximately 48 by 36 feet. Construction of an airport in the Lake of the Ozarks State Park began in 1967 amid controversy. The controversy subsided but construction continued…The airport* [is] *to be known as the Lee C. Fine Memorial Airport, honoring a former director of the State Park Board.*

Local business leaders were optimistic, and one noted, "We actually feel this will be a major airport in this part of the country."

Chapter 19

1. Davidson's appeal in the 1960s may have been aided by the perception that he was a "Western" singer, a format that had a wider acceptance at that time than "country" music due to the popularity of the "singing cowboy" performers of the previous decades.
2. This confuses catfish, which are generally bait-fished, with spoonbill (also known as "paddlefish"), which must be "snagged" (or netted).

Chapter 20

1. In general, although the true local population had no choice but accept the changes wrought by the coming of the lake, it would be misstatement to characterize that acquiescence as the positive acceptance of change required for development and economic progress.

   The growing year-rounder population of the late twentieth and early twenty-first centuries represented a greater threat to the locals than did the tourists or the influx of workers and professionals associated with the construction and operation of the dam. Over the course of decades, there gradually came to be a new mix of population and demographic profiles. Also, summer tourists and weekenders did not vote in local elections and historically had shown little interest in the governments of the area. However, a year-rounder permanent population is eligible to vote—a fact not lost on the true locals and their political culture.

Of great interest should be the term "summer shack" and its probable original source, the previously cited December 14, 1931 *Time* magazine article—here excerpted for its historical interest and also contrast to the plainer journalistic language of latter times:

> *A dragon will crawl across future maps of Missouri. Its head will be at Bagnell, in the central part of the state. Its tail and claws will twist 129 mi. westward. It will be labeled Lake of the Ozarks, largest artificial lake in the world, created by a dam built by Stone & Webster for Union Electric Light & Power Co. (North American subsidiary). St. Louisans and Kansas Citizens will have summer shacks and duck shooting lodges along its 1,300 mi. of shore line. St. Louisans, who will consume a large part of the dam's annual 425 million kilowatt hours of electricity, also hope that Lake of the Ozarks will temper their city's blistering summers.*

So go contemporary reports. The Lake of the Ozarks was created for the sole benefit of city folk, their recreation at "summer shacks and duck shooting lodges" on the lake and their air-conditioned and electric-lighted housing back home. Union Electric and other big "grid" operators had no interest in the rural market. However, the result of this indifference was the founding of one of the most successful government-sponsored enterprises: rural electric cooperatives.

What needs attention here, though, is the apparent attitude of the American general culture reflected in the magazine article. The true locals of the Ozarks did not matter in the creation of the lake. They would receive no service from the dam turbines and uncertain benefit from the recreational or occupational opportunities offered by the world's "largest artificial lake."

2. In the rear view, the period looks to be a movement toward the Branson model by the Osage Beach operators, but this is apparent only from a historical perspective. Osage Beach was not destined to sustain the live music entertainment model of Branson.

3. (KVL) My observation in transitional economic development always demonstrated that a successful transition is led by champions. By the 1980s, the Branson area had its champions firmly in place, while the Lake of the Ozarks had begun to lose some of its important boosters, men like the Four Season's Koplar, Mace, Dennis Hilton and Burt Duenke (the Tan-Tar-A founder). A characteristic all champions share is that of the positive acceptance of change. This is the first step in effecting new economic and social development, particularly when change is as dramatic as that which the Lake of the Ozarks region has experienced over the decades.
4. The fact is that the twentieth-century Lake of the Ozarks promoters' commercial push for both permanent and vacation home residents and for appeal to tourism was greatly successful. For much of the final decades of that era, the lake consistently polled as one of the top ten tourist destinations for such areas in the country, drawing a reported 3.5 million visitors annually. One report noted, "40% of people who own a second home in Missouri, own it at the Lake of the Ozarks…additionally the Lake is becoming one of the fastest growing retirement communities in the Midwest."

   Also touted (in 2015) were "world class boating, watersports and 15 golf resorts…restaurants, shoreline nightclubs and bars, lodging, resort facilities, family recreation facilities…and…the state's largest factory outlet mall"—all of which describes precisely the vision of the decades of champions of the Lake of the Ozark whose determination and struggle seem to have created a remarkable and uniquely American community from beginnings that could once only have been viewed as "highly problematical." Ceil Abbott, "Interesting Tidbits about Lake of the Ozarks," *The Lake Today*, September 2, 2015.

Conclusion

1. (DWP) A passing note of a new occupational opportunity that emerged in the Ozarks (and Missouri) in the twentieth century—legal moonshine. Generally speaking (ignoring the Prohibition-era anomaly), from a cultural point of view, moonshine is most often associated with social activities—the jug is shared, the dance commences or the coon hunt progresses, and so on. In the Ozarks, such socialization and the ensuing alcohol consumption has historically been common with little stigma attached.

In the twenty-first century, a number of legal moonshine operations had sprung up in much of the Ozark territory, which is to say the operators paid taxes and submitted to government inspection and regulation. Sometime early in the second decade, I interviewed the owner of the Ozark Distillery, LLC, in Osage Beach (www. ozarkdistillery.com).

After selling me a jug of one-hundred-proof corn whiskey of his own manufacture and giving me a tour of the still and bottling rooms, owner Dave Huffman asked if I thought his was the first legal still in Camden County. I told him I believed that might be so. I cannot say for sure, but first or not, his product was mighty smooth sipping.

Appendix B

1. While our initial interest in this subject was spurred from the mention of "sundown towns" by a few informants, we soon decided a brief examination of the history of the black experience in the Ozarks was warranted.

Gerard Schultz wrote, "The vast majority of settlers in the Northern Ozarks did not have slaves. In 1840 only 41 of the 337 families in Miller County had slaves. Of these, 21 families had only one slave each and the remainder had from two to nine slaves."

Schultz noted that in 1860, the slave population in Morgan County was 649; in Miller County, 238; and Camden County, 206. If current demographic information is desired, search "Office of Social and Economic Data Analysis," http://www.oseda.missouri.edu

Kremer and Orr employed the term "Colored People." Whatever the terminology, there is no question that the subject resorts were intended by their founders and owners to maintain racial separation.

As our thoughts developed in this book, we had extensive discussion on the use of the word "Negro." We recognized the actual term has and is undergoing various levels of acceptance. The U.S Census tabulated population race by "Negro." It wasn't until 2013, as noted in a February 25, 2013 *New York Post* article, entitled "Census to Replace 'Negro' with 'Black' or 'African-American'" that the U.S. Census Bureau announced the change of replacing "Negro" with black or African-American as a race category. http://nypost.com/2013/02/25/census-to-replace-negro-with-black-or-african-american.

On the subject of racial attitudes, as noted, the Ozarks have historically been dominated by white people, and in spite of the relatively sparse population of minorities, there were said to have been numerous "sundown towns" in the region. Any speculation on the matter would be anecdotal, and it should be noted that most Ozarkers of the twenty-first century would almost certainly not (or barely) acknowledge the existence of these towns, past or present. Those harkening back to the story of the Japanese designer at the Lodge of the Four Seasons who reportedly was badly beaten by locals must be mindful that a likely cause of the incident was the fact that less than two decades had passed since World War II.

Appendix C

1. The Missouri Fish Commission began a trout stocking program in 1878. The program was haphazardly administered until 1937, when the Missouri Department of Conservation (MDC) was established. The MDC "restricted trout stocking to cold water streams in three state parks and five other trout management areas open to public fishing" (Wes Swee and Tom Whelan, "It's Easy to Get Hooked," *Missouri Conservationist* 75, no. 3, March 2014). Another large species—striped bass—also must be stocked since the construction of the Truman Dam. http://www.stripers247.com/Missouri-striper-fishing.php.

SELECTED BIBLIOGRAPHY

Repository

National Archive and Records Administration: RG 103, entry 1052, Box 4, folder #1 (W.J. Dwyer, Jr.)

Articles and Books

Angel, Traci. *The Scars of Project 459: The Environmental Story of the Lake of the Ozarks*. Fayetteville: University of Arkansas Press, 2014.

Bartram, Dorothy, ed. *Versailles Missouri: Its First One Hundred Fifty Years*. Commemorative booklet. Versailles, MO: Versailles Commerce League, 1985.

Bennett, Victor W. "Joint Stock Land Banks in Retrospect." *Journal of Farm Economics* 20, no. 4 (November 1938). Published by Agricultural and Applied Economics Association.

Columbia Daily Tribune. "Technology Offers Clues into New Madrid Fault." October 8, 2013.

Dohm, Richard R. "Political Culture of Missouri." In *Missouri Government and Politics*, edited by Richard J. Hardy, Richard R. Dohm and David Leuthold, chapter 2. Columbia: University of Missouri Press, 1995.

Edmonson, Samantha. "10 Questions with Ha Ha Tonka State Park's Nancy Masterson." *The Lake Today*, June 19, 2013.

Feeler, Heather. "Missouri Loses a True Forest Pioneer." *Missouri Conservationist* 76, no. 7 (July 2015).

Focus: A Weekly Newspaper Serving the Heart of the Lake since 1987. "Reader's Mailbag." October 24, 2012.

Gallaher, Art, Jr. *Plainville: Fifteen Years Later.* New York: Columbia University Press, 1961.

Gist, Noel P., and Sylvia Fleis Fava. *Urban Society.* 6th ed. New York: Harper and Row, 1974.

Growth in the Heartland: Challenges and Opportunities for Missouri. Washington, D.C.: The Brookings Institution Center for Urban and Metropolitan Policy, 2002.

Hagey, Paul. "The Mosaic of an Ozark Forest." *Missouri Conservationist* 72, no. 3 (March 2011).

Hall, Leonard. *Possum Trot Farm: An Ozark Journal.* St. Louis, MO: Caledonia Press, 1949.

History of Morgan County Missouri, 1833–1978. Versailles, MO: Morgan County Historical Society, 1979 (Vol. 1) and 2009 (Vol. 2).

Hubbell, Victoria Pope. *A Town on Two Rivers: A History of Osage Beach, Missouri.* Published by the City of Osage Beach, 1998.

Jeffries, T. Victor. *Before the Dam Water: Story and Pictures of Old Linn Creek, Ha Ha Tonka and Camden County.* Springfield, MO: Midwest Litho and Publishing, 1974.

Kremer, Gary R., and Evan P. Orr. *Race and Meaning.* Columbia: University of Missouri Press, 2014.

Larsen, Eric. *A Nation Gone Blind: America in an Age of Simplification and Deceit.* Emeryville, CA: Shoemaker and Hoard, 2006.

Lewis, Paula Alexander, comp. "A Look Back." *Eldon (MO) Advertiser,* September 18, 2014.

Marshall, Howard Wight. *Play Me Something Quick and Devilish: Old-Time Fiddlers in Missouri.* Columbia: University of Missouri Press, 2012.

McMillen, Margot. *The Golden Lane: How Missouri Women Gained the Vote and Changed History.* Charleston, SC: The History Press, 2011.

Nickel, Wally, ed. *From These Beginnings: Ozarks Past, Book One.* Camdenton, MO: Lake of the Ozarks Council of Local Governments Historical Presentation Program, 1981.

Nocera, Joe. "Fannie, Freddie Deserve More Credit." *New York Times.* Repr., *Columbia Daily Tribune,* August 18, 2013.

Ostmann, Barbara Gibbs. "Underwater Fun." *Rural Missouri: A Monthly Publication of the Missouri Electric Cooperatives* 65, no. 10 (October 2013).

Peek, Dan William. *Live at the Ozark Opry.* Charleston, SC: The History Press, 2010.

Rafferty, Milton. *The Ozarks: Land and Life*. Fayetteville: University of Arkansas Press, 2001.

Randolph, Vance. *Ozark Superstitions*. New York: Columbia University Press, 1947.

Rayburn, Otto Ernest. *Ozark Country*. New York: Duell, Sloan and Pearce, 1941.

Rhodes, Richard, and the editors of Time-Life Books. *The Ozarks*. New York: Time-Life Books, 1974.

Schultz, Gerard. *Early History of the Northern Ozarks*. N.p., 1937.

Shoreline Management Plan/Osage Project, FERC No. 459.

Singer, Dale. "'Simple' Hancock Amendment Spawned Complex State Finances." *St. Louis Beacon*, April 8, 2011.

"Tall Tales, Windies and Just Plain Lies." *Hoosier Folklore Bulletin* 1, no. 1 (June 1942): 12–22.

Tindall, George Brown, with David E. Shi. *America: A Narrative History*. 3rd ed. New York: W.W. Norton, 1992.

Van Landuyt, Kent Bruce. "Social Change in the Missouri Ozarks from 1930 through 1960." Central Missouri State College, 1971.

Weaver, H. Dwight. *History & Geography of Lake of the Ozarks*. Vol 1. Eldon, MO: Osage River Trails, 2005.

———. *Lake of the Ozarks: The Early Years*. Charleston, SC: Arcadia Publishing, 2000.

West, James. *Plainville, U.S.A.* New York: Columbia University Press, 1945.

Williams, Bill, and Dorothy Williams, comp. "History of Versailles and Morgan County." Unpublished manuscript.

INDEX

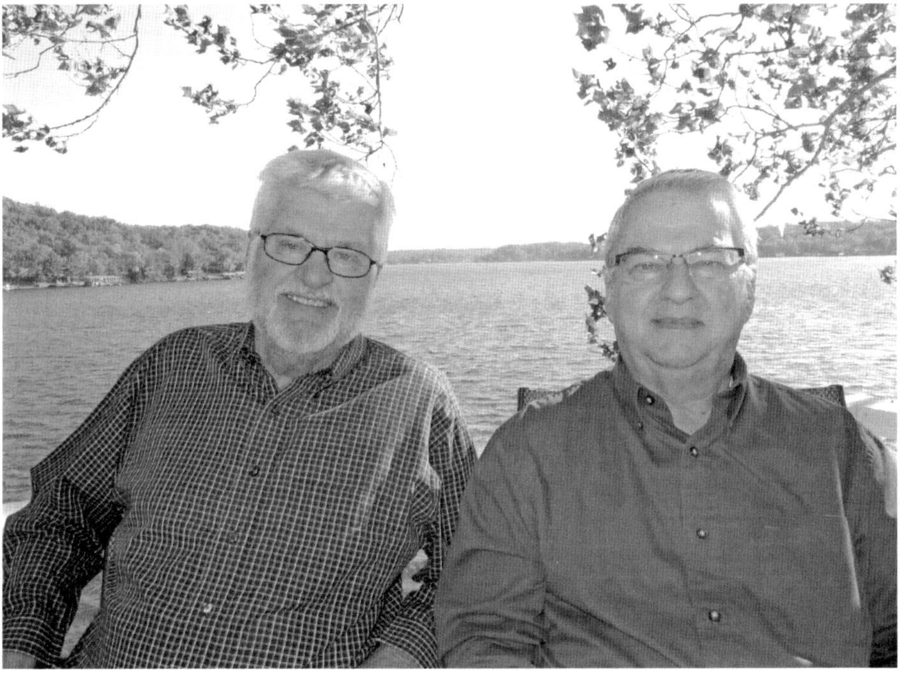

ABOUT THE AUTHORS

Kent Van Landuyt, a lifelong resident of the Ozarks, has over forty years in public service as a sociologist and planner with the state of Missouri and was selected by the 108th and 109th U.S. Congresses as a Congressional Fellow to provide analysis and advice on issues relating to transportation and national economic development. His master's thesis at the University of Central Missouri provided the foundation for this book. Kent lives with his wife, Alice, on a peaceful homestead near Eldon, Missouri—"The gateway to the Lake of the Ozarks."

Dan William Peek, an Ozark native, is a marketing consultant, banjo player and writer who lives with his wife, Joy, in a first-tier house on the Gravois arm of the Lake of the Ozarks. Dan is the author of numerous articles, essays and editorials and two previous books, *To the Point: The Story of Darts in America* and *Live! At the Ozark Opry* (the latter published by The History Press in 2010). Dan is co-founder and executive director of Grandparents and Others on Watch, Inc., a nonprofit child advocacy organization. Dan and Joy were classmates of Kent Van Landuyt in the Morgan County RII school system (Versailles, Missouri), but the opportunity to co-author a book did not arise until some decades later. The resulting product is well worth the wait.